B O O K   4

English
No Problem!

Kathryn Quinones
Office of Adult and Continuing Education
New York City Department of Education, NY

Donna Korol
Office of Adult and Continuing Education
New York City Department of Education, NY

New Readers Press

English—No Problem! ™
English—No Problem! Level 4 Student Book
ISBN 1-56420-359-X

Copyright © 2004 New Readers Press
New Readers Press
Division of ProLiteracy Worldwide
1320 Jamesville Avenue, Syracuse, New York 13210
www.newreaderspress.com

Printed in the United States of America
9 8 7 6 5 4 3 2 1

All proceeds from the sale of New Readers Press materials
support literacy programs in the United States and worldwide.

Acquisitions Editor: Paula L. Schlusberg
Developer: Mendoza and Associates
Project Director: Roseanne Mendoza
Project Editor: Pat Harrington-Wydell
Content Editor: Judi Lauber
Production Director: Heather Witt-Badoud
Designer: Kimbrly Koennecke
Illustrations: Carolyn Boehmer, Linda Tiff
Production Specialist: Alexander Jones
Cover Design: Kimbrly Koennecke
Cover Photography: Robert Mescavage Photography
Photo Credits: Hal Silverman Studio

Authors

Kathryn Quinones
Office of Adult and
   Continuing Education
New York City Department
   of Education, NY

Donna Korol
Office of Adult and
   Continuing Education
New York City Department
   of Education, NY

Contributors

National Council Members
Audrey Abed, *San Marcos Even Start Program, San Marcos, TX*
Myra K. Baum, *New York City Board of Education (retired), New York, NY*
Kathryn Hamilton, *Elk Grove Adult and Community Education, Sacramento, CA*
Brigitte Marshall, *Oakland Adult Education Programs, Oakland, CA*
Teri McLean, *Florida Human Resources Development Center, Gainesville, FL*
Alan Seaman, *Wheaton College, Wheaton, IL*

Reviewers
Sabrina Budasi-Martin, *William Rainey Harper College, Palatine, IL*
Linda Davis-Pluta, *Oakton Community College, Des Plaines, IL*
Patricia DeHesus-Lopez, *Center for Continuing Education, Texas A&M University, Kingsville, TX*
Gail Feinstein Forman, *San Diego City College, San Diego, CA*
Carolyn Harding, *Marshall High School Adult Program, Falls Church, VA*
Trish Kerns, *Old Marshall Adult Education Center, Sacramento City Unified School District, Sacramento, CA*
Debe Pack-Garcia, *Manteca Adult School, Humbolt, CA*
Pamela Patterson, *Seminole Community College, Sanford, FL*
Catherine Porter, *Adult Learning Resource Center, Des Plaines, IL*
Jean Rose, *ABC Adult School, Cerritos, CA*
Eric Rosenbaum, *Bronx Community College Adult Program, Bronx, NY*
Laurie Shapiro, *Miami-Dade Community College, Miami, FL*
Terry Shearer, *North Harris College Community Education, Houston, TX*
Abigail Tom, *Durham Technical Community College, Chapel Hill, NC*

Pilot Teachers
Connie Bateman, *Gerber Adult Education Center, Sacramento, CA*
Jennifer Bell, *William Rainey Harper College, Palatine, IL*
Marguerite Bock, *Chula Vista Adult School, Chula Vista, CA*
Giza Braun, *National City Adult School, National City, CA*
Sabrina Budasi-Martin, *William Rainey Harper College, Palatine, IL*
Wong-Ling Chew, *Citizens Advice Bureau, Bronx, NY*
Renee Collins, *Elk Grove Adult and Community Education, Sacramento, CA*
Rosette Dawson, *North Harris College Community Education, Houston, TX*
Kathleen Edel, *Elk Grove Adult and Community Education, Sacramento, CA*
Margaret Erwin, *Elk Grove Adult and Community Education, Sacramento, CA*
Teresa L. Gonzalez, *North Harris College Community Education, Houston, TX*
Fernando L. Herbert, *Bronx Adult School, Bronx, NY*
Carolyn Killean, *North Harris College Community Education, Houston, TX*
Elizabeth Minicz, *William Rainey Harper College, Palatine, IL*
Larry Moore, *Long Beach Adult School, Long Beach, CA*

Kathryn Powell, *William Rainey Harper College, Palatine, IL*
Alan Reiff, *NYC Board of Education, Adult and Continuing Education, Bronx, NY*
Brenda M. Rodriguez, *San Marcos Even Start, San Marcos, TX*
Juan Carlos Rodriguez, *San Marcos Even Start, San Marcos, TX*
Joan Siff, *NYC Board of Education, Adult and Continuing Education, Bronx, NY*
Susie Simon, *Long Beach Adult School, Long Beach, CA*
Gina Tauber, *North Harris College, Houston, TX*
Diane Villanueva, *Elk Grove Adult and Community Education, Sacramento, CA*
Dona Wayment, *Elk Grove Adult and Community Education, Sacramento, CA*
Weihua Wen, *NYC Board of Education, Adult and Continuing Education, Bronx, NY*
Darla Wickard, *North Harris College Community Education, Houston, TX*
Judy Wurtz, *Sweetwater Union High School District, Chula Vista, CA*

Focus Group Participants
Leslie Jo Adams, *Laguna Niguel, CA*
Fiona Armstrong, *New York City Board of Education, New York, NY*
Myra K. Baum, *New York City Board of Education (retired), New York, NY*
Gretchen Bitterlin, *San Diego Unified School District, San Diego, CA*
Patricia DeHesus-Lopez, *Center for Continuing Education, Texas A&M University,
    Kingsville, TX*
Diana Della Costa, *Worksite ESOL Programs, Kissimmee, FL*
Frankie Dovel, *Orange County Public Schools, VESOL Program, Orlando, FL*
Marianne Dryden, *Region 1 Education Service Center, Edinburgh, TX*
Richard Firsten, *Lindsey Hopkins Technical Center, Miami, FL*
Pamela S. Forbes, *Bartlett High School, Elgin, IL*
Kathryn Hamilton, *Elk Grove Adult and Community Education, Sacramento, CA*
Trish Kerns, *Old Marshall Adult Education Center, Sacramento City Unified School
    District, Sacramento, CA*
Suzanne Leibman, *The College of Lake County, Grayslake, IL*
Patti Long, *Old Marshall Adult Education Center, Sacramento City Unified School
    District, Sacramento, CA*
Brigitte Marshall, *Oakland Adult Education Programs, Oakland, CA*
Bet Messmer, *Santa Clara Adult School, Santa Clara, CA*
Patricia Mooney, *New York State Board of Education, Albany, NY*
Lee Ann Moore, *Salinas Adult School, Salinas, CA*
Lynne Nicodemus, *San Juan Adult School, Carmichael, CA*
Pamela Patterson, *Seminole Community College, Sanford, FL*
Eric Rosenbaum, *Bronx Community College, Bronx, NY*
Linda Sasser, *Alhambra District Office, Alhambra, CA*
Federico Salas, *North Harris College Community Education, Houston, TX*
Alan Seaman, *Wheaton College, Wheaton, IL*
Kathleen Slattery, *Salinas Adult School, Salinas, CA*
Carol Speigl, *Center for Continuing Education, Texas A&M University, Kingsville, TX*
Edie Uber, *Santa Clara Adult School, Santa Clara, CA*
Lise Wanage, *CASAS, Phoenix, AZ*

Special thanks to Eric Rosenbaum for help in the development of this book.

About This Series

Meeting Adult Learners' Needs with *English—No Problem!*

English—No Problem! is a theme-based, performance-based series focused on developing critical thinking and cultural awareness and on building language and life skills. Designed for adult and young adult English language learners, the series addresses themes and issues meaningful to adults in the United States.

English—No Problem! is appropriate for and respectful of adult learners. These are some key features:

- interactive, communicative, participatory approach
- rich, authentic language
- problem-posing methodology
- project-based units and task-based lessons
- goal setting embedded in each unit and lesson
- units organized around themes of adult relevance
- contextualized, inductive grammar
- student materials designed to fit into lesson plans
- performance assessment, including tools for learner self-evaluation

Series Themes

Across the series, units have the following themes:
- Life Stages: Personal Growth and Goal Setting
- Making Connections
- Taking Care of Yourself
- Personal Finance
- Consumer Awareness
- Protecting Your Legal Rights
- Participating in Your New Country and Community
- Lifelong Learning
- Celebrating Success

At each level, these themes are narrowed to subthemes that are level-appropriate in content and language.

English—No Problem! Series Components

Five levels make up the series:
- literacy
- level 1 (low beginning)
- level 2 (high beginning)
- level 3 (low intermediate)
- level 4 (high intermediate)

The series includes the following components.

Student Book

A full-color student book is the core of each level of *English—No Problem!* Literacy skills, vocabulary, grammar, reading, writing, listening, speaking, and SCANS-type skills are taught and practiced.

Teacher's Edition

Each teacher's edition includes these tools:
- general suggestions for using the series
- scope and sequence charts for the level
- lesson-specific teacher notes with reduced student book pages
- complete scripts for all listening activities and Pronunciation Targets in the student book

Workbook

A workbook provides contextualized practice in the skills taught at each level. Activities relate to the student book stories. Workbook activities are especially useful for learners working individually.

 This icon in the teacher's edition indicates where workbook activities can be assigned.

Reproducible Masters

The reproducible masters include photocopiable materials for the level. Some masters are unit-specific, such as contextualized vocabulary and grammar activities, games, and activities focusing on higher-level thinking skills. Others are generic graphic organizers. Still other masters can be used by teachers, peers, and learners themselves to assess the work done in each unit.

Each masters book also includes scripts for all listening activities in the masters. (Note: These activities are *not* included on the *English—No Problem!* audio recordings.)

 This icon in the teacher's edition indicates where reproducible masters can be used.

Audio Recording

Available on CD and cassette, each level's audio component includes listening passages, listening activities, and Pronunciation Targets from the student book.

This icon in the student book and teacher's edition indicates that the audio recording includes material for that activity.

Lesson-Plan Builder

This free, web-based *Lesson-Plan Builder* allows teachers to create and save customized lesson plans, related graphic organizers, and selected assessment masters. Goals, vocabulary lists, and other elements are already in the template for each lesson. Teachers then add their own notes to customize their plans. They can also create original graphic organizers using generic templates.

When a lesson plan is finished, the customized materials can be printed and stored in PDF form.

This icon in the teacher's edition refers teachers to the *Lesson-Plan Builder,* found at www.enp.newreaderspress.com.

Vocabulary Cards

For literacy, level 1, and level 2, all vocabulary from the Picture Dictionaries and Vocabulary boxes in the student books is also presented on reproducible flash cards. At the literacy level, the cards also include capital letters, lowercase letters, and numerals.

Placement Tool

The Placement Test student booklet includes items that measure exit skills for each level of the series so that learners can start work in the appropriate student book. The teacher's guide includes a listening script, as well as guidelines for administering the test to a group, for giving an optional oral test, and for interpreting scores.

Hot Topics in ESL

These online professional development articles by adult ESL experts focus on key issues and instructional techniques embodied in *English—No Problem!*, providing background information to enhance effective use of the materials. They are available online at www.enp.newreaderspress.com.

Addressing the Standards

English—No Problem! has been correlated from the earliest stages of development with national standards for adult education and ESL, including the NRS (National Reporting System), EFF (Equipped for the Future), SCANS (Secretary's Commission on Achieving Necessary Skills), CASAS (Comprehensive Adult Student Assessment System) competencies, BEST (Basic English Skills Test), and SPLs (Student Performance Levels). The series also reflects state standards from New York, California, and Florida.

About the Student Books

Each unit in the student books includes a two-page unit opener followed by three lessons (two at the literacy level). A cumulative unit project concludes each unit. Every unit addresses all four language skills—listening, speaking, reading, and writing. Each lesson focuses on characters operating in one of the three EFF-defined adult roles—parent/family member at home, worker at school or work, or citizen/community member in the larger community.

Unit Opener Pages

Unit Goals The vocabulary, language, pronunciation, and culture goals set forth in the unit opener correlate to a variety of state and national standards.

Opening Question and Photo The opening question, photo, and caption introduce the unit protagonists and engage learners affectively in issues the unit explores.

Think and Talk This feature of levels 1–4 presents questions based on classic steps in problem-posing methodology, adjusted and simplified as needed.

What's Your Opinion? In levels 1–4, this deliberately controversial question often appears after Think and Talk or on the first page of a lesson. It is designed to encourage lively teacher-directed discussion, even among learners with limited vocabulary.

Picture Dictionary or Vocabulary Box This feature introduces important unit vocabulary and concepts.

Gather Your Thoughts In levels 1–4, this activity helps learners relate the unit theme to their own lives. They record their thoughts in a graphic organizer, following a model provided.

What's the Problem? This activity, which follows Gather Your Thoughts, encourages learners to practice another step in problem posing. They identify a possible problem and apply the issue to their own lives.

Setting Goals This feature of levels 1–4 is the first step of a unit's self-evaluation strand. Learners choose from a list of language and life goals and add their own goal to the list. The goals are related to the lesson activities and tasks and to the unit project. After completing a unit, learners revisit these goals in Check Your Progress, the last page of each workbook unit.

First Lesson Page

While the unit opener sets up an issue or problem, the lessons involve learners in seeking solutions while simultaneously developing language competencies.

Lesson Goals and EFF Role The lesson opener lists language, culture, and life-skill goals and identifies the EFF role depicted in that lesson.

Pre-Reading or Pre-Listening Question This question prepares learners to seek solutions to the issues presented in the reading or listening passage or lesson graphic that follows.

Reading or Listening Tip At levels 1–4, this feature presents comprehension and analysis strategies used by good listeners and readers.

Lesson Stimulus Each lesson starts with a reading passage (a picture story at the literacy level), a listening passage, or a lesson graphic. A photo on the page sets the situation for a listening passage. Each listening passage is included in the audio recording, and scripts are provided at the end of the student book and the teacher's edition. A lesson graphic may be a schedule, chart, diagram, graph, time line, or similar item. The questions that follow each lesson stimulus focus on comprehension and analysis.

Remaining Lesson Pages

Picture Dictionary, Vocabulary Box, and Idiom Watch These features present the active lesson vocabulary. At lower levels, pictures often help convey meaning. Vocabulary boxes for the literacy level also include letters and numbers. At levels 3 and 4, idioms are included in every unit.

Class, Group, or Partner Chat This interactive feature provides a model miniconversation. The model sets up a real-life exchange that encourages use of the lesson vocabulary and grammatical structures. Learners ask highly structured and controlled questions and record classmates' responses in a graphic organizer.

Grammar Talk At levels 1–4, the target grammatical structure is presented in several examples. Following the examples is a short explanation or question that guides learners to come up with a rule on their own. At the literacy level, language boxes highlight basic grammatical structures without formal teaching.

Pronunciation Target In this feature of levels 1–4, learners answer questions that lead them to discover pronunciation rules for themselves.

Chat Follow-Ups Learners use information they recorded during the Chat activity. They write patterned sentences, using lesson vocabulary and structures.

In the US This feature is a short cultural reading or brief explanation of some aspect of US culture.

Compare Cultures At levels 1–4, this follow-up to In the US asks learners to compare the custom or situation in the US to similar ones in their home countries.

Activities A, B, C, etc. These practice activities, most of them interactive, apply what has been learned in the lesson so far.

Lesson Tasks Each lesson concludes with a task that encourages learners to apply the skills taught and practiced earlier. Many tasks involve pair or group work, as well as follow-up presentations to the class.

Challenge Reading

At level 4, a two-page reading follows the lessons. This feature helps learners develop skills that prepare them for longer readings they will encounter in future study or higher-level jobs.

Unit Project

Each unit concludes with a final project in which learners apply all or many of the skills they acquired in the unit. The project consists of carefully structured and sequenced individual, pair, and group activities. These projects also help develop important higher-level skills such as planning, organizing, collaborating, and presenting.

Additional Features

The following minifeatures appear as needed at different levels:

One Step Up These extensions of an activity, task, or unit project allow learners to work at a slightly higher skill level. This feature is especially useful when classes include learners at multiple levels.

Attention Boxes These unlabeled boxes highlight words and structures that are not taught explicitly in the lesson, but that learners may need. Teachers are encouraged to point out these words and structures and to offer any explanations that learners require.

Remember? These boxes present, in abbreviated form, previously introduced vocabulary and language structures.

Writing Extension This feature encourages learners to do additional writing. It is usually a practical rather than an academic activity.

Technology Extra This extension gives learners guidelines for doing part of an activity, task, or project using such technology as computers, photocopiers, and audio and video recorders.

Contents

Unit 1: Taking the First Step .10

- ◆ Vocabulary: Goal-setting words • Problem-solving words
- ◆ Language: Compare present perfect and simple past (review) • Compare present perfect and past perfect
- ◆ Pronunciation: Intonation with statements • Intonation with *yes/no* questions
- ◆ Culture: Changing jobs

Lesson 1	Planning for Success	.12
Lesson 2	Learning from the Past	.15
Lesson 3	Living Up to Your Potential	.18
Challenge Reading	Personal Development Classes	.21
Unit 1 Project	Write a Letter to Yourself from the Future	.23

Unit 2: Selling Your Skills .24

- ◆ Vocabulary: Interview words • Words for feelings
- ◆ Language: Conditional contrary to fact • Indirect speech
- ◆ Pronunciation: Sentence stress • Vowel sounds in *say, said,* and *says*
- ◆ Culture: Expected behavior in the workplace

Lesson 1	With a Little Help from My Friends	26
Lesson 2	What Do I Do Now?	29
Lesson 3	Getting the Word Out	32
Challenge Reading	Business Customs: How Should You Act?	35
Unit 2 Project	Make a Personal Achievement Record	37

Unit 3: Getting Help .38

- ◆ Vocabulary: Words for offering and asking for help • Words for talking about difficult issues
- ◆ Language: Objects of prepositions • Prepositional phrases
- ◆ Pronunciation: *of* after a word ending in a consonant • Holding over final consonants
- ◆ Culture: Getting professional help

Lesson 1	Sharing Your Problems	40
Lesson 2	Identifying Resources	43
Lesson 3	Substance Abuse: Problems and Solutions	46
Challenge Reading	Action Plans: How to Fight Domestic Abuse and Substance Abuse	49
Unit 3 Project	Make a Resource Guide	51

Unit 4: On Your Own .52

- ◆ Vocabulary: Words about small businesses • Words related to safety
- ◆ Language: Connecting ideas with *so, because,* and *although* • *who, which,* and *that* in adjective clauses
- ◆ Pronunciation: *-tion* ending • Reductions with *have*
- ◆ Culture: Independence as a cultural value

Lesson 1	Becoming Your Own Boss	54
Lesson 2	Doing the Paperwork	57
Lesson 3	Safety First	60
Challenge Reading	Small Business Report	63
Unit 4 Project	Create a Business	65

Unit 5: Think before You Buy! .66

- ◆ Vocabulary: Words that consumers need
- ◆ Language: Present and past participles used as adjectives • Embedded questions
- ◆ Pronunciation: Stress in compound nouns
- ◆ Culture: Technology and progress

Lesson 1	Shopping Smart	68
Lesson 2	Doing the Research	71
Lesson 3	Consumer Rights and Consumer Awareness	74
Challenge Reading	Let the Buyer Beware	77
Unit 5 Project	Create a Class Consumer Guide	79

Unit 6: Protecting Your Rights 80

◆ Vocabulary: Legal terms
◆ Language: Adverbs of time with the past perfect • Special problems with prepositions, articles, gerunds, and infinitives
◆ Pronunciation: Consonant blends
◆ Culture: Written and verbal contracts

Lesson 1   Read the Fine Print! 82
Lesson 2   Taking Legal Action 85
Lesson 3   Speaking Up for Your Rights 88
Challenge Reading Service Contracts and Extended Warranties 91
Unit 6 Project   Create a Personal Legal Glossary 93

Unit 7: Participating in Your Community 94

◆ Vocabulary: Language for participating in a democracy
◆ Language: Present and past participles used as adjectives • Past participles of irregular verbs
◆ Pronunciation: Disappearing /h/ of function words
◆ Culture: Tradition of self-reliance and community involvement

Lesson 1   Participating in Elections 96
Lesson 2   Keeping Informed 99
Lesson 3   Getting Involved 102
Challenge Reading Why I Became an American Citizen 105
Unit 7 Project   Make a Community Resource Guide 107

Unit 8: It's Never Too Late 108

◆ Vocabulary: Words for giving a speech • Words about ways to learn
◆ Language: Past continuous • Past perfect continuous
◆ Pronunciation: Disappearing sounds and syllables
◆ Culture: Learning at any age

Lesson 1   What Works Best for You? 110
Lesson 2   Working Out the Details 113
Lesson 3   Showing Your Pride 116
Challenge Reading Adult Learning Styles 119
Unit 8 Project   Find Your Personal Learning Style 121

Unit 9: Celebrating Success 122

◆ Vocabulary: Words for resumes • Words for job interviews
◆ Language: Passive voice in simple present (review) • Verb tenses (review)
◆ Pronunciation: Diphthongs • Syllable stress
◆ Culture: Personal qualities admired in the US

Lesson 1   Making the Most of Yourself 124
Lesson 2   Making Your Work History Count 127
Lesson 3   Making a Good Impression 130
Challenge Reading Ask Annabelle 133
Unit 9 Project   Prepare a Resume 135

Listening Scripts 136
US Map 141
World Map 142
Topics 143
Grammar and Pronunciation 144

Taking the First Step

Looking to the Future

Community
1

Home
2

Work/School
3

◆ **Vocabulary** Goal-setting words • Problem-solving words

◆ **Language** Compare present perfect and simple past (review) • Compare present perfect and past perfect

◆ **Pronunciation** Intonation with statements • Intonation with *yes/no* questions

◆ **Culture** Changing jobs

I came to the US to build a good life for myself and my family.

She had clear goals for her future, and she reached those goals.

Did you ever ask an older family member to tell you about his or her life?

Patria's grandmother has had a long and interesting life. She has predicted that Patria will be happy and successful. Patria wants to believe this, but sometimes she fears she will never reach her goals.

Think and Talk

1. What do you see in the picture? What are Patria and her grandmother doing?
2. How do you think Patria feels about her grandmother's life?
3. Are you influenced by what you know about your family members' experience, goals, and ideas? Explain why or why not.

Gather Your Thoughts

There are many ways to accomplish what you want in your life. Some people wait to see what will happen. Others seem to know what to do. In your group, decide which of the following is most important in reaching your goals:

- luck
- knowing somebody who can help you
- hard work
- having a plan and following it
- something else (Identify what it is.): _____

Report to the class about your choice. Give reasons.

What's the Problem?

Look at the answers that you and your classmates thought were the most important in reaching your personal goals. What stops people from reaching their goals? What do people need to do to reach their goals?

Setting Goals

Read the list of goals below. Then write another goal that is important to you. Rank the goals in order from 1 (most important) to 6.

_____ **a.** identify my most important goals

_____ **b.** learn how to make a plan for reaching my goals

_____ **c.** learn to use problem-solving techniques

_____ **d.** be able to use past perfect, present perfect, and simple past appropriately

_____ **e.** use appropriate intonation with questions and statements

_____ **f.** another goal: _____

Meet with people who made the same number 1 choice. Discuss the reasons for your choice. Calculate what percentage of the class made the same choice that you did. Report back to the class.

Vocabulary

Circle new words. Brainstorm meanings and sample sentences. Take notes. List other words that you want to learn.

accomplish

clarify

predict/prediction

details

long-term goals

short-term goals

success/successful

appropriate

Idiom Watch!

taking the first step

Planning for Success

◆ Clarify your personal goals

◆ Compare present perfect with simple past

| botanical garden |
| botanist |
| diploma |
| herbs |

How did coming to the US affect your dreams and goals?

◆ **Listening Tip** 🎧 A good way to understand what you hear is to practice focused listening—listening for a specific type of information. One way to focus your listening is to take notes. Listen to Patria and her grandmother talk. Give them your full attention. Listen for what they say about their dreams. Write a few words to help you remember what you hear. The listening script is on page 136.

Idiom Watch!

a dream come true
dead-end job
take a chance

Patria and her grandmother are talking about their dreams.

Talk or Write

1. Patria's grandmother had dreams. What were they? What are Patria's dreams?

2. How did the grandmother's dreams change? Why did they change?

3. How can dreams be helpful in reaching goals? In addition to dreaming, what else does Patria say you need to do?

4. What is one goal you dream of reaching? What plan do you have for reaching that goal?

Partner Chat   Talk with a partner. Ask these questions:
- Have you ever achieved an important goal by first dreaming and then making specific plans? What was it?
- In what ways has the reality been better or worse than your dream?

Record your partner's answers on an idea map like the one below.
- In the left circle, write one or more ways the reality has been better than your partner dreamed.
- In the right circle, write one or more ways the reality has been worse than your partner dreamed.
- In the middle circle, record one or more things that have happened exactly as your partner dreamed and planned them.

Vocabulary

Circle new words. Brainstorm meanings and sample sentences. Take notes. List other words that you want to learn.

achieve

dream

imagine

reality

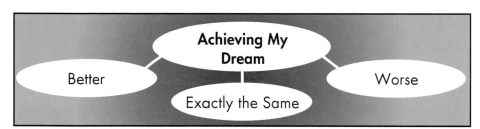

Achieving My Dream

Better

Exactly the Same

Worse

Grammar Talk: Comparing Simple Past with Present Perfect

<u>Simple Past</u>	<u>Present Perfect</u>
Grandmother's husband **gave** her a music box.	Grandmother **has listened** to the music for 50 years.
Patria **studied** hard in high school.	Patria **has dreamed** of going to college since then.

Compare the simple past sentences with the present perfect sentences. How are the verbs different? Which verbs talk about something that happened at a specific time in the past? Which talk about something that happened at an unspecified time or times in the past and is continuing? With your class, write a rule for using simple past. Write another rule for using present perfect. What verb form is used with have *or* has *in the present perfect?*

Activity A   With a partner, ask and answer questions about things you have done. Have you ever asked an older family member to tell you about his or her life? Have you ever looked at photos with an older family member? Have you ever dreamed of improving your life? With your partner, write one or two questions to ask other group members.

Have you ever asked an older family member to tell you about his or her life?

Yes, I have.

Who did you ask? What did that person tell you?

I asked my uncle to tell me how he came to this country.

Activity B **Partner Chat Follow-Up** Look at your Partner Chat idea map from page 13. In your notebook, answer these questions about your goals and your partner's goals.

- What important goal have you achieved by dreaming and planning? What about your partner?
- In which ways has the outcome of your goal been better than expected? What about your partner's goal?
- In which ways has the outcome of your goal been worse than expected? What about your partner's goal?

Activity C Try dreaming about your future for a few moments. Sit comfortably and close your eyes. Relax for a moment. Try to focus your mind. Your teacher will read these questions to you.

- It is 10 years from now. You have your dream job. You are at your workplace. What kind of place is it? An office? Hospital? Store? Someplace else?
- What are you doing?
- Are you alone or with other people? If you are with others, are you the boss or an employee? What are the other people doing?
- Where are you living? What is your city or community like?

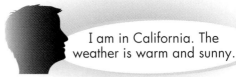

I am in California. The weather is warm and sunny.

Now tell a partner about your dream job. Try to imagine yourself at the job. Add more details if you want.

One Step Up
In your notebook, write a short paragraph about your dream job. Include a main idea and supporting details. Tell why you are happy in the job.

 TASK 1: Make a Plan for Your Future

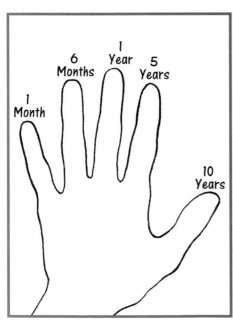

As a first step to planning, set some long- and short-term goals. Draw an outline of your hand on a piece of paper.

- At the top of your little finger, write "1 Month." On the finger, write something that you would like to achieve in one month.
- On the top of your ring finger, write "6 Months." On the finger, write something that you would like to achieve in six months.
- At the top of your middle finger write "1 Year." On the finger, write something that you would like to achieve in one year.
- At the top of your index finger, write "5 Years." On the finger, write something that you would like to achieve in five years.
- At the top of your thumb write "10 Years." On the thumb, write something that you would like to achieve in 10 years.

Work fast. Let your feelings guide you. Tell your group about some of your goals.

Learning from the Past

◆ Think about your past experiences

◆ Compare present perfect with past perfect

| experience |
| record |

What have you learned from other people's experiences?

◆ **Reading Tip** Think of time lines you have seen in other places. What kind of information do they usually provide?

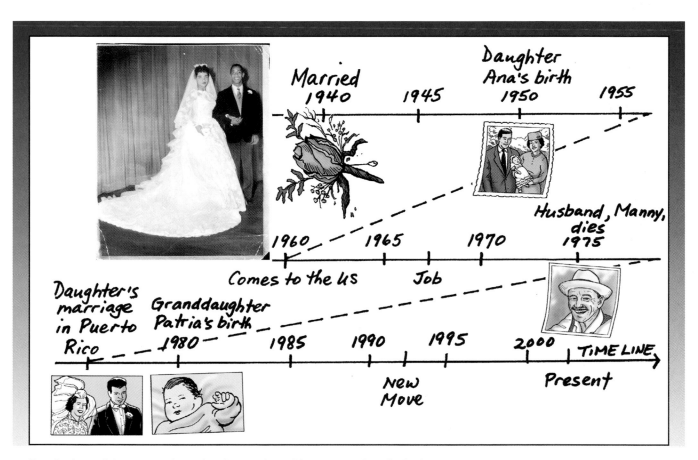

Patria loved her grandmother's stories. She wanted to help her grandmother record her life history. She worked with her grandmother to make a time line showing the most important events of her life.

Talk or Write

1. What did you learn about Patria's grandmother's life from her time line?
2. What kinds of events are important to Patria's grandmother?
3. If you had to make a time line of your own life, what five to eight main events would you include? Write notes in your notebook. You will use these notes later.

Pronunciation Target • Intonation with *Yes/No* Questions

🎧 *Intonation is the rising and falling tone of your voice. Good intonation makes speech sound more interesting and easier to understand. Listen to your teacher or the audio.*

Have you ever been to a baseball ↑ game?
Have they arrived ↑ yet?

What did you hear? Generally when the expected answer in English is yes *or* no, *the speaker's voice goes up a little at the end of a question.*

Vocabulary

Circle new words. Brainstorm meanings and sample sentences. Take notes. List other words that you want to learn.

event

experience

dare

fulfill

Class Chat With a partner, choose one question from the list below. Take turns asking at least 10 people in your class the question. Ask them to explain their answers. Record names and answers on a chart like the one below. Make your voice go up at the end of questions.

One Step Up
If you get a *no* answer to question 1, 2, or 4, ask if the person has done that activity yet.

1. Had you studied English before you came to the US?
2. Had you driven a car before you turned 16?
3. Had you met the teacher before you started this class?
4. Had you seen a baseball game before you came to the US?

One-Question Interview

Your Question: _____

Name	Answer	Student said?

Grammar Talk: Compare Present Perfect and Past Perfect

Present Perfect	Past Perfect
I **have learned** that mistakes are necessary in life.	I **had made** many mistakes before I dared to ask for help.
He **has accomplished** his goal.	He **had accomplished** his goal before he came to the US.
They **have worked** here for six weeks.	I **had worked** for six weeks when my boss called me into his office.

Compare the present perfect sentences with the past perfect sentences. Think about when the action takes place. The present perfect sentences show action occurring at an indefinite time in the past or action that continues on into the present. The past perfect sentences show action completed before another event in the past.

Activity A Class Chat Follow-Up Look at your Class Chat chart from page 16. What did you learn about your classmates? Write sentences in your notebook.

Luz had studied English before she came to the US.

She had studied it for three years in high school.

Activity B Think of older people you have known. What things did you learn from them? Make a list of five things you learned. Share your list with your group.

My grandmother taught me about my family history.

Now use your list to write sentences in the past perfect.

Before my grandmother died, she had taught me about my family history.

Activity C Think about one person you wrote about in Activity B. Write a short note to that person. Thank the person for helping you. Use the opening lines shown to the right, or write your own.

Now copy your note onto nice paper. If possible, send the note to the person.

> Dear_____,
>   I've been thinking about you and what you have taught me.
>   I would like you to know that I will always remember when you taught me_____
> _____
> Thank you,

One Step Up
Read your note to your group. The group can ask you questions.

Activity D Ask someone you admire about strategies for success. Choose someone that you consider successful—maybe a family member, teacher, or professional. Ask, "How did you plan to reach your goal? What is one dream that you have fulfilled in your life?" Take notes and give a brief presentation to your group.

 TASK 2: Make a Time Line

Make a time line of your own life. Begin with your birth. Add at least five important points in your life. Use the notes you made for Talk or Write on page 15. Continue your time line 10 years into the future by adding events that you want to happen. Use the time line at the beginning of this lesson as a model. Be creative. Add tape, ribbons, photographs, or magazine pictures to your time line. Use your completed time line as an outline, and make notes for a short presentation to your class about yourself. Try to talk about each point on your time line. Use present perfect and past perfect when you can.

I had been married for two years when my daughter was born.

I have lived in three states since I came to the US.

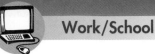

Living Up to Your Potential

◆ Talk about job or career goals

◆ Learn about changing jobs in the US

Do you need perfect English to reach your goals?

◆ **Reading Tip**   Good readers use their experience and knowledge to evaluate what they read. Read about Patria's goals and plans. Use your own experience and knowledge to decide if you agree or disagree with what she says.

stuck

frustrated

guide

peppermint

spearmint

> I was in the Garden yesterday during my break. A guide was talking to a group of children. He gave them incorrect information about the plants. He said that spearmint and peppermint are the same. I wanted to say something, but my English is not good enough. I felt so frustrated! Why is English so difficult?

> I am ready to take action to achieve my goals. My short-term goal is to become a guide at the Garden. I think I would like that job for a few years. My long-term goal is the goal I've always had — to become a botanist. Can I ever reach that goal? Is it possible for me to go to college? I need perfect English, don't I?

> My grandmother taught me to love and understand plants and to use them to make people healthy. Even when I was a little girl, I had dreamed of becoming a botanist. I wanted to study botany in the university in Puerto Rico. Then we came to the US. Now I'm stuck working here in the cafeteria because I can't speak English well!

Idiom Watch!

live up to

take action

That's not right! Should I say something?

Patria has worked at the cafeteria in the Botanical Garden for two years. Jack, her co-worker, attends college. He and Patria write short letters to help her practice English. Here are paragraphs from some of Patria's letters.

Talk or Write

1. Patria wrote, "I am ready to take action to achieve my goals." Do you think she is really ready?
2. Patria did not say anything to the guide. She wrote, "My English is not good enough." Was that a good reason? Why or why not?
3. Patria wrote: "Why is English so difficult?" Do you agree that English is a difficult language? Why or why not?
4. Patria wrote to Jack, "Is it possible for me to go to college? I need perfect English, don't I?" Do you agree with her? Why or why not?

In the US ★ Changing Jobs

It's common for people in the US to change jobs and careers. If someone is feeling stuck in a job or frustrated with a career, that person may quit, go back to school, and try to find work in a different profession. People in the US sometimes take personality and aptitude tests to help them discover the best career for them. Career counselors offer these tests and recommend careers that fit people's interests, skills, and needs.

☞ Compare Cultures

Changing jobs and careers, reading books by career advisors, visiting career counselors, and taking personality and aptitude tests are common activities in the US, but not everywhere. Tell group members about experiences you or a family member have had changing jobs or finding a new career in another country. What was similar to what happens in the US? What was different? Which do you prefer?

Vocabulary

Circle new words. Brainstorm meanings and sample sentences. Take notes. List other words that you want to learn.

- aptitude
- career
- frustrated
- personality
- potential
- profession
- stick/stuck

Pronunciation Target • Intonation with Statements

🎧 Intonation, the ↑ rising and ↓ falling of the speaker's voice, is one thing that makes English sound like English. When Americans talk, does the tone of their voices sound flat and steady, or does it seem to go up and down? Listen to your teacher or the audio.

If you don't know where you're ↑ go ↓ ing, you'll probably never ↑ get ↓ there.
I like to visit the botanical ↑ gar ↓ den.
Ca ↑ reer counselors advise people on ca ↑ re ↓ ers.

Did you notice how the voice goes up and down at the end of phrases and sentences?

Activity A   Write three statements about your goals. Trade papers with your partner. Read your partner's sentence out loud. Put an arrow for the up and down intonation at the end of your partner's sentences. Your partner will do the same with yours. Do you agree? Your teacher will listen to you read your sentences to each other.

✂🖥 Technology Extra

Search the Internet for information about a career that interests you. For example, look for career information at your state's Department of Labor web site. Write three useful facts from the information you read. Share your information with your group.

Activity B   Use a chart like the one below to interview your classmates about great jobs. Follow these steps:

exaggerate

- Ask each person's name and write it in the column under Name.
- Ask the person to name a really great job. Write that job in the column under Job.
- Ask the reason the person would love that job. Write it in the column under Reason.

Name	Job	Reason

Repeat the steps with as many classmates as you can interview. When you finish, meet with your group and talk about these great jobs. As a group, decide which is the best one. Together, write a short description of the job. You can exaggerate to make the job sound really wonderful. Have one member of the group report back to the class.

Activity C   With your group, role-play an interview for the wonderful job your group chose in Activity B. First give names to the interviewer and the applicant. Prepare questions for the interview. Write down answers to the questions. Practice walking in the door, shaking hands, and so on. Have fun preparing, and then act it out for the class. After each group's role-play, classmates can suggest ways to make performances and intonation better.

One Step Up

With a partner, write your role-play. Read it, and correct spelling and grammar. Trade papers with another pair. Make suggestions to help each other's writing. Collect the role-plays in a class booklet.

TASK 3: Plan and Take Action

One way to turn a dream into reality is to make a plan for achieving your goals. Look at one of the long-term goals (for 5 years or 10 years) from your hand chart on page 14. Work with your group to think of one thing that you could do this week to move closer to that goal. Use this process:

- One student completes the statement "I want to . . ." with a long-term goal from Lesson 1.
- Other group members complete the statement "You could . . ." with one action to take this week.
- Group members discuss the suggestions, decide on the most useful one, and recommend it.
- The first student accepts the suggestion or replaces it with a better one.
- Repeat these steps with each student in the group.

In five years I want to have a job with a future.

This week you could call a school for their catalog.

In your notebook, write your own long-term goal and the action to take this week. Report to the class on the results of your action.

◆ **Reading Tip**   When you read, do you use a dictionary to look up every word that you don't know? If you do, you may read slowly, and this makes reading less enjoyable. You can often guess the meaning of a new word or new idiom by the way it's used in a sentence or a paragraph. This is called *finding meaning from context*. Look at the reading below for some examples. For example, what do you think the word *social* means in the first course description? Where do you think people would go for social dancing?

Personal Development Classes

Adults can take personal development classes through community colleges, religious organizations, and even public schools. Most personal development classes are inexpensive, and some are even free.

Some adult learners recently took personal development classes at a community college. They described their reasons for taking these classes and the skills that they learned:

Social Dancing   I have never been satisfied with my dancing skills. I wanted to relax and become more sociable. I learned the most popular dances, including line dances and several types of Latin dances. The atmosphere was friendly and comfortable. I had been embarrassed to dance in public. Now, I've developed a lot of confidence. I am not afraid that people are laughing at me when I dance.

The Power of Your Will   I have never been able to make up my mind about what to do with my life. I've had many ideas and plans, but few results. I wanted to learn how to set goals for myself. After taking this workshop, I understood the meaning of willpower. Having this ability to set goals for myself and stick to them is very important. Now each day I do at least one thing to move toward my goal.

Acting   Since I was a child, I have aspired to be an actor. I had always wanted to find out if I really had the talent. In this course, I acted with other students in scenes from popular plays. I studied characters and did acting exercises. Our class presented a play at a senior citizens center. They loved it! I loved it too.

Buying Your Own Home   I've often dreamed of buying my own home, but I was afraid I could never do it. I wanted to learn about the process of home buying. This course didn't give me every detail about buying a home, but it gave me essential information about how to become a homeowner.

Swimming for Beginners   Although I have lived near beautiful beaches since I was a child, I was afraid to go into the water. For years, I had wanted to overcome my fear of water. The instructor taught me to relax my mind and my body in the water. I still haven't learned to be an Olympic swimmer, but I enjoy swimming now. I'm sure that everyone who takes this course will learn to swim—and learn to enjoy swimming!

Introduction to Computers   I had never touched a computer before I took this course. I was afraid of computers because they looked so intimidating. This hands-on course, where we spent every minute in front of the computers, changed my attitude. I've already learned some basic programs, and I have my own e-mail account. I communicate with friends and relatives in my home country by e-mail. I also e-mail my new friends from computer class. I plan to continue taking computer classes. I'm sure my new skills will also help me find a better job.

How to Start Your Own Business   I had worked in many jobs, but I'd never gotten along with my bosses. I wanted to work in a job without a boss. That's why I decided to start my own business. I knew that in my own business, I could be my own boss. This course taught me that starting your own business requires patience and hard work. It also gave me practical information about signing contracts and getting insurance.

Talk or Write

1. How did the person who wrote about Social Dancing change her life? Do you know of anyone whose life is better because of a personal development class? What happened?
2. Give one or more examples of classes that changed the writers' attitudes. How did each class change that writer's attitude?
3. List some words from the reading that were new to you. Share your list with a partner. What things in the reading helped you understand the new words?

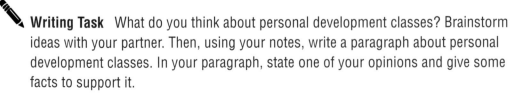 **Writing Task**   What do you think about personal development classes? Brainstorm ideas with your partner. Then, using your notes, write a paragraph about personal development classes. In your paragraph, state one of your opinions and give some facts to support it.

Write a Letter to Yourself from the Future

Imagining your life in the future can help you plan and work to achieve your goals. Write a letter from yourself in the future to yourself in the present.

Get Ready

Start with the goals that you listed for Task 1, the time line that you made for Task 2, and the long-term goal and steps that you discussed for Task 3.

1. Draw another personal time line starting today and ending in 10 years. Include your short-term and long-term goals. Also include any good suggestions for steps you should take.
2. Cut out pictures from magazines to illustrate your future work, home, family, and community. Cut out want ads, information on courses, and other material that can help you take steps you plan.
3. Paste the cutouts to show where you want to be in 10 years and what you will do between now and then. You can also draw pictures.

Do the Work

Pick a specific time between now and 10 years from now on your personal time line. Write a three-paragraph letter to yourself from that time in the future. Follow these directions for your letter from the future you to the present you. Use the form your teacher gives you.

1. On the first line, write *Dear* [your first name].
2. Next, imagine you have achieved some of your goals. Write a draft of a paragraph about your new life. Use the illustrations from your time line to help you add details. Where are you? Home? Office? What kind of place do you live in? What is your family like? What are your hobbies? Write this paragraph in the present and present perfect tenses.
3. Now, write a draft of a paragraph about the steps that you took to achieve your goals up to that time. Write this paragraph in the past tense.
4. Next, write a draft of a paragraph with advice about the steps you should take to reach the rest of your goals by the end of the 10 years. Write in the present tense. Use the word *should*.

Present

Read your letter to a partner and listen to your partner read his or her letter. Show your letter to your teacher. Ask for suggestions to help your writing. Then revise your letter.

One Step Up
Write an answer from the present you to the future you.

Selling Your Skills

Presenting Your Skills

Home
1

Work/School
2

Community
3

◆ **Vocabulary** Interview words • Words for feelings

◆ **Language** Conditional contrary to fact • Indirect speech

◆ **Pronunciation** Sentence stress • Vowel sounds in *say, said,* and *says*

◆ **Culture** Expected behavior in the workplace

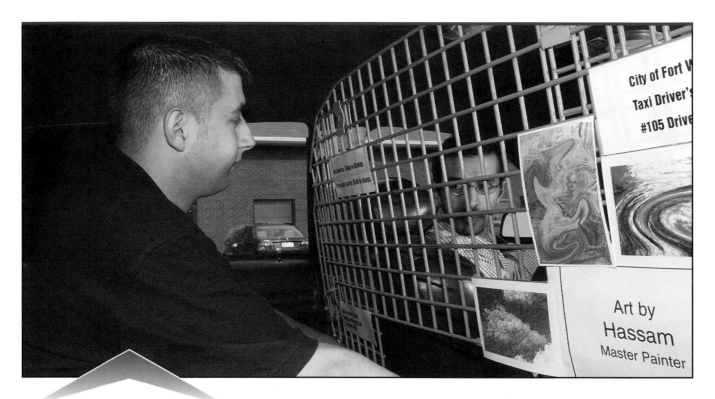

When have you found work by telling people about things you can do well?

Hassam Ahmad is from Egypt. He drives a taxi for ABC Taxi, but he wants to be an artist. He wants to meet customers. He also wants to meet someone who will help him sell his work. He puts photos of his artwork in the taxi for his passengers.

Think and Talk

1. What do you see in the picture? What is Hassam doing?
2. Does Hassam like his job? How do you know? What other work does he like?
3. How is Hassam telling people about his skills and his work? Is this a good idea? Explain your answer. What else could he do?
4. Do you like talking about and showing your skills? Why or why not?

What's Your Opinion? Is it right for Hassam to try to sell his work in the taxi when working for his employer? Explain your answer.

Gather Your Thoughts Hassam is trying to sell his art, but it is difficult. He hopes to meet someone who can help him. The photos in his taxi help him network, or talk to people about his work.

Do you network, or talk to people, to solve problems or deal with challenges? Ask yourself these questions:

- Have you asked for advice or information in the past week? In the past month? Who did you ask? What did you ask?
- Who has asked *you* for help or advice in the past month?

With your group, list the kinds of people you network with. Make an idea map. Here's an example:

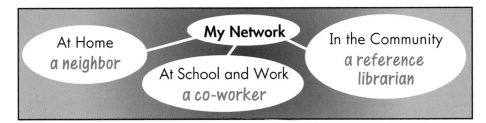

What's the Problem? Look at your idea map. What problems could stop you from networking? Shyness? Not enough friends? Not enough time? Your English? Talk with a partner or think about these questions.

Setting Goals Read the list of goals below. Then write another goal that is important to you. Rank the goals in order from 1 (most important) to 6. Give reasons for your choices.

_____ **a.** network to deal with challenges

_____ **b.** improve my English so I can do well in a job interview

_____ **c.** understand everyday conversation

_____ **d.** be able to ask for and give advice

_____ **e.** become good at talking about my skills or my work

_____ **f.** another goal: _____

Tally goals for the class. What percentage of people thought that each goal was most important?

Vocabulary

Circle new words. Brainstorm meanings and sample sentences. Take notes. List other words that you want to learn.

advice

challenge

network

shy/shyness

skill

Idiom Watch!

deal with

With a Little Help from My Friends

◆ Talk about your skills

◆ Use conditional contrary to fact

Who can give you advice about jobs, your plans, and your future?

◆ **Listening Tip** 🎧 If you know how the speaker feels, it's easier to understand the message. Through networking in his cab, Hassam has met someone who wants to interview him about his art. A friend gives him advice about how to prepare for his interview. Is Hassam worried? Tense? Excited? Does he feel some other way? Try to identify the tone of Hassam's voice in this conversation. The listening script is on page 136.

ingredients

label

professional

Idiom Watch!

go well

make a good impression

present yourself

Hassam and his wife, Masa, are talking with their friend Peter.

Talk or Write
1. How does Hassam feel about this meeting with Ms. Patterson? How do you know?
2. What does Peter mean when he says, "We never have enough time."
3. Hassam and Masa invited Peter to help Hassam prepare for an important interview. Was that a good idea? Why or why not?

Class Chat   Think about people who can give you advice. Walk around. Ask questions. Organize your answers in a chart like the one below.

If you needed advice about renting an apartment, who would you talk to?

To my sister-in-law. She works at a real estate company.

If you needed advice about _____, who would you talk to?

What's your name?	About what?	Who?
Patricia	renting an apartment	my sister-in-law

Vocabulary

Circle new words. Brainstorm meanings and sample sentences. Take notes. List other words that you want to learn.

- professional
- resume
- suggestion
- tone
- tense
- worry/worried

Grammar Talk: Conditional Contrary to Fact

If I **were** rich, I **would sing** all day. *OR*
I **would sing** all day if I **were** rich.

If he **had** time, he **would deal with** the problem. *OR*
He **would deal with** the problem if he **had** time.

Look at the verb tenses in the main clauses and the if *clauses. Talk about what you noticed with your classmates and your teacher.*

Did you notice that in all the sentences, the order of the main clauses and the if *clauses can be reversed?*

*Did you notice that the sentences all tell about possibilities, not facts? They are contrary-to-fact sentences. The verb in the main clause in each sentence is the conditional (*would + base form*). The verb in the* if *clause is in the past tense.*

Remember?

Present Conditional

If he **has** time, he **will deal with** the problem. *OR*
He **will deal with** the problem if he **has** time.

Did you notice these things?

- *The sentence tells about something that might happen in the future.*
- *The order of the main clause and the if clause can be reversed.*

Activity A   With a partner, write the letter of the *if* clause that should follow
each main clause. Then put a check mark in front of the contrary-to-fact sentences.
Be careful! Only one *if* clause matches each main clause.

_____ **1.** Hassam will make a better impression

_____ **2.** Hassam wouldn't be so nervous

_____ **3.** Peter would give suggestions

_____ **4.** Ms. Patterson will try to sell Hassam's work

_____ **5.** Hassam and Masa would take a vacation

    a. if Hassam asked for help.

    b. if Peter helps him.

    c. if she likes his photos.

    d. if he were ready for the interview.

    e. if they had more money.

Activity B   **Class Chat Follow-Up** Look at your Class Chat chart. Write about
three group members. Who would they talk to if they needed advice?

1. <u>Patricia would talk to her sister-in-law, Tania.</u>

2. _____

3. _____

4. _____

Activity C   Think about a time when you wanted to make a good first impression
and present yourself well. Was it a job interview? An open house at your child's
school? A special party? Describe that experience to a partner. Your partner will
ask you the questions in the chart below. Then switch roles.

Questions	Answers
When did you want to make a good impression?	When I talked to our teacher for the first time.
What happened?	I only said two words.
If you did it again, what would you do differently?	I would not act so shy.

One Step Up

Write your answers to the three
questions in your notebook. Read
your answers to the group. Then
each group member says how he
or she would deal with that same
situation. Say, "If that happened to
me, I would ____."

 TASK 1:   Asking the Right Questions

Look at the kinds of people that your group listed in the idea map on page 25.
Think about asking them questions. If you could ask questions to help deal with
your challenges, what would you ask? Use these four categories: Work, Personal,
Financial, Educational. Write the questions in your notebook.

<u>Work: How can I ask for a pay raise?</u>

What Do I Do Now?

◆ Talk about how to act in an interview

◆ Learn about US business and social customs

Have you ever had a job interview? How did you feel?

annoyed

body language

receptionist

◆ **Reading Tip**   When you read the conversation below between Hassam and Peter, think about the time of each action. What happened to Hassam first? What happened next? Then what happened?

Idiom Watch!

just make it

After the Interview

"Well, you know I was a little nervous about the interview. I left early so I wouldn't be late, but I got lost. I wasn't late, but I just made it.

"I thought that the woman who greeted me was the receptionist, so I asked her to tell Ms. Patterson that I was there. I was pretty embarrassed when she said *she* was Ms. Patterson. She held out her hand and I just looked at it. Then I realized that she expected me to shake hands."

"Well, Hassam, I've been in this country all my life, and I'm still sometimes confused about what to do in an interview."

"Yeah? Anyway, I asked her if she wanted to see some pictures of my work. She looked a little annoyed and said that we should sit down first. I didn't think I should sit down before she did, but she was pointing at the chair. I just sat down. I thought I should say something, so I asked how she liked the weather. She frowned a little, and it was easy to read that body language! She asked if I had some pictures to show her. Luckily I had my photos. After that, I relaxed. She said my work was excellent and well-organized. She could see I was prepared.

"She chose two pieces to try to sell in her shop. She wants to come to our apartment and see the rest of my work. You know what? Now I'm more worried than before! What if I make more mistakes?"

"It sounds like you'll be fine."

Talk or Write

1. What happened to Hassam before he got to the gallery? How do you think he felt?

2. When did Hassam offer to show pictures of his art? Why did Ms. Patterson look annoyed?

3. Why was Hassam still worried after the interview?

In the US Business Customs

In general, people in the US act quite formal in business situations. However, some businesses are more informal. For that reason, it's often difficult to know exactly how to act in business situations. Here are some things you can do.

If you are going to have an interview with a company, get all the information you can about that company from books, web sites, and people. Network with friends, classmates, and acquaintances, especially US-born people. Don't forget the library. Ask the librarian to help you find a book on business customs. In any business situation, watch what other people are doing. They can be models for the way you act.

☞ Compare Cultures

Preparing a resume, researching a company, and interviewing for a job are common activities in the US, but not everywhere. Tell the class about experiences you or a family member had looking for a job in another country. What was similar? What was different? Which ways of finding jobs do you prefer?

Vocabulary

Circle new words. Brainstorm meanings and sample sentences. Take notes. List other words that you want to learn.

> body language
>
> custom
>
> situation
>
> annoyed
>
> confused
>
> embarrassed
>
> formal
>
> informal

Idiom Watch!

handle yourself

Pronunciation Target • Sentence Stress

🎧 *Listen to your teacher or the audio. Listen for the stressed words in the sentences.*

> If I **needed** a **book,** I'd **go** to the **library.**
> If I **wanted** a **job,** I'd **ask** my **brother** for **help.**

In English, you need to stress the right words to be understood. English speakers usually stress content words—the words that carry meaning. Those words sound a little longer and clearer than others. Did you hear the stress on the words in bold type? Say the sentences with a partner. Check each other's pronunciation.

Activity A Read the sentences below. Underline the stressed words. Practice with a partner. Listen carefully to your partner. Do you agree about which words should be stressed?

- If I had more time, I would work on my project.
- If I needed advice, I would ask my sister-in-law.
- If Peter hadn't helped Hassam, his interview wouldn't have gone so well.

Now write three sentences of your own with *if* clauses. Then do the same activity again with your partner.

Activity B What social or business customs and situations in the US are confusing to you? In your group, list all the confusing situations you can. One person will write the group list on the board. When all groups have listed their situations, one student from each group will count how many students are confused in each situation. Make a class list of the 10 most confusing situations from all the lists.

Activity C With a partner, pick one of the confusing situations from Activity B. Think about how you and your partner would handle yourselves in that situation. Try to find something that you both would do. Then find something that neither of you would do. Complete a four-section square like the one below.

I	Both of Us
If I was worried about how to divide the check, I would ask the other person for help.	If we were worried about how to divide the check, both of us would ask the waiter for separate checks.
Neither of Us	**My Partner**
If we were worried about how to divide the check, neither of us would act nervous.	If Ricardo was worried about how to divide the check, he would pay for both of us.

Eating in restaurants with people from the US is sometimes confusing. I am worried about how to divide the check.

Activity D With your group, sit in a circle. Tell a story about a person who went to a job interview and made a lot of mistakes. Each person in the circle can add a sentence with a new mistake to the story. You can make the story funny. One person in the group writes the story. Another person reads the story to the class.

One Step Up
With your group, role-play the story you write for your class. Remember to stress content words when you speak. Ask your classmates to suggest better ways to act in an interview.

TASK 2: Make a List of US Social and Business Customs

Make a list of suggestions that could be helpful to someone coming to the US. Include *do's* and *don'ts* about US business and social customs. Here are some examples:

Do: Stand when you are introduced to someone.

Don't: Don't be late for an interview. Give yourself extra time.

🖥 Technology Extra
Combine all the ideas from the lists into one brochure. Use a computer to write and design your brochure. Give a copy to other classes at your school.

Getting the Word Out

◆ Understand how to use problem-solving skills to get a better job

◆ Use indirect speech

advertise

flyer

unique

Could you advertise your work this way? Why or why not?

◆ **Reading Tip**   When you read, look for the main idea. As you read this flyer, ask
yourself, "What is the most important thing that Hassam is trying to communicate?"

Idiom Watch!
get the word out

Art by Hassam
You're invited to see some exciting paintings!

Place: Patterson Artworks
Address: 240 S. Wayne Ave.
                    Fort Worth

Come see the paintings!
Take home a unique piece of art!

ABOUT THE ARTIST
Hassam Ahmad is from Cairo.
As a student, he won two prizes for his art in his city.
He is a skilled new artist who is already well-known
in Cairo for his work.

Talk or Write
1. What information does Hassam give in the flyer?
2. Is anything missing? What other information could you include in this
   flyer?
3. What does Hassam want people to do when they read this flyer? Do
   you think he achieved his goal?
4. What does the flyer say about Hassam's skills and abilities? Why do
   you think he included this information?

Group Chat Talk about your own talents, abilities, and skills. Work in groups of four. Change roles so that you can practice each sentence and be a listener. Complete a chart like the one below with your group.

Name	What can you do?	Report it.
Ana	I can fix cars.	Ana said that she could fix cars.

Grammar Talk: Indirect Speech

Direct:		Hassam said, "I **want** to take **my** paintings to the shop."
Indirect:	Present:	Hassam **says** that he **wants** to take **his** paintings to the shop.
	Past:	Hassam **said** that he **wanted** to take **his** paintings to the shop.

When do you use indirect speech? What happens to the verb and the pronoun when the sentence changes from direct to indirect speech? Look at the extra punctuation marks in the direct speech sentence. What are they? Why are they used?

Pronunciation Target • Vowel Sounds in *Say, Said,* and *Says*

🎧 *Listen to your teacher or the audio. Notice that the letter* a *has a different sound in* say *than in* says *and* said.

We **say** that we can help make a poster.
Maria **says** that she can design web sites.
Koji **said** that he could type.

Activity A   Group Chat Follow-Up Write sentences in your notebook about things three of your classmates can do. Use direct and indirect speech. Use information from your Group Chat chart.

<u>Ana can fix cars. She said that she could fix cars.</u>

Activity B In your group, one person reads the sentences. The others repeat. Then take turns using indirect speech to tell what someone said.

1. Masa said, "I think you should use a flyer."
2. They said, "We want to see your paintings."
3. Ms. Patterson said, "I like your work."
4. Peter said, "I'm still sometimes confused about what to do in an interview."
5. Hassam said, "I really want to sell my work."

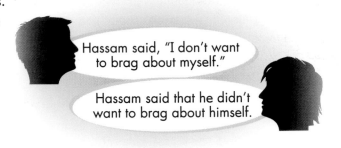

Hassam said, "I don't want to brag about myself."

Hassam said that he didn't want to brag about himself.

Activity C On page 29, Hassam used reported speech to tell Peter about his interview with Ms. Patterson. With a partner, write and role-play the interview using direct speech. Be creative.

Activity D Ask your partner about an interview experience. It could be a job interview, a citizenship interview, a talk with a school official, and so on. You can also talk about an interview someone else had. Use the following questions. When you finish, your partner will interview you.

One Step Up
Use your answers to Activity D to write about your interview or your partner's interview.

1. What was the purpose of the interview?
2. When was your interview?
3. What did you wear?
4. Where was the interview?
5. Who was the person you met? Do you remember the person's name or job title?
6. Do you remember any questions you had to answer? What were they?
7. How did it feel to talk about yourself?
8. What was the most difficult part of the interview?
9. If you could do or say anything differently, what would it be?
10. What did you learn from your interview?

 TASK 3: Present a Collage of Your Skills and Achievements

Plan a presentation for the class about your skills and achievements. Make a collage of pictures and words from magazines or newspapers as part of your presentation. Choose pictures and words that show your skills and achievements. Add small objects. Show the collage as you tell the class about your skills. These questions may help you:

• Which of these skills do I use in my current job or in daily life?
• Which skills would I like to use in my future jobs or in daily life?

◆ **Reading Tip**   Reading an article quickly to find out what it is about or see how it is organized is a strategy many good readers use. Scanning, or doing a quick first reading, can help you get a general idea of what you will read. Later you can read the article again carefully for details. Read this article on business customs quickly. As you read, think about how the writer organized the ideas. Then read again more slowly and carefully before answering the questions on page 36.

Business Customs: How Should You Act?

How should you act at the workplace in the US? Customs for the workplace are always changing. For example, a few years ago, men and women were often treated differently at work. Today many men and women expect to be treated the same in the workplace, although in reality this does not always happen. Here are a few tips to help you avoid mistakes in the world of work.

Opening Doors   Many men are confused about when to hold a door open for a woman. At work, a man should hold a door for a woman if he would hold it for a man in the same situation.

The following "rules" are true for both men and women:
- Hold the door open for a superior, male or female.
- Hold the door for anyone, male or female, who is carrying a lot of things.
- Hold the door for anyone, male or female, who is hurt or needs your help.

What about revolving doors? Since the person in front does all the pushing, you should enter the door ahead of a person in one of the categories above (a superior, a person carrying packages, or someone in need of help). And, of course, push the revolving door carefully so you don't hurt anyone.

Shaking Hands   Both men and women shake hands in the same way in the workplace. Here's how it's done:
- Extend your right hand. It doesn't matter who extends a hand first.
- Look into the other person's eyes. This is called *making eye contact.*
- Present yourself as a serious but friendly person. You don't need to smile, but if you do, your smile should be sincere.
- Clasp the other person's hand. Apply some pressure, but not too much or too little. Practice makes perfect. Ask an American friend to check your handshake. Too much pressure? Too little? Keep practicing.
- Move your clasped hands up and down once or twice, and then let go. Easy? Now you know how to shake hands for business in the US.

Is this any different from shaking hands socially? Well, a little. First of all, remember that at the workplace, it doesn't matter who extends a hand first. In social situations, this is still true when two women or two men shake hands. However, when a woman and a man shake hands socially, for example at a party or in a restaurant, the man should wait for the woman to extend a hand first. What if the woman doesn't extend a hand? That's easy. You don't shake hands. Just smile politely and keep the conversation going.

Standing and Sitting If you are in your own work area, you should stand to greet a visitor. You may also stand to meet a superior who you don't see every day—for example, the company president. This is done regardless of the gender of either person. In another person's office, wait to be invited to sit. If it's your space, don't forget to invite your visitor to sit.

This rule works another way. If you are very busy and don't have time for a long conversation, it's OK not to invite your visitor to sit. Your conversation will probably be shorter, and you will both be able to go back to work sooner.

The Golden Rule is the same everywhere: Treat other people the way you would like to be treated.

clasp

disability

extend

gender

regardless

revolving

superior

treat

Idiom Watch!

Practice makes perfect.

Talk or Write

1. What are the writer's main points about manners in a business situation?
2. Give one or more examples from the article of appropriate manners in a business situation.
3. What does the writer say about differences between business manners and social manners?

Writing Task In your notebook, write a one-paragraph summary of the article. Summarize what the article says about business manners. Do this by listing the three areas that the article mentions. For each area, write about how to act in a business situation.

Make a Personal Achievement Record

All people have to present their skills and achievements at one time or another. Be organized and prepare to brag about your achievements. Do this by keeping a record of your achievements and skills. Have it ready for times when you need to talk about yourself—an interview, a promotion review, a school application, or other important events.

> update
>
> up-to-date

Get Ready

1. Start with the list of skills and achievements you prepared for Task 3. Use the checklist your teacher gives you.
2. Buy a loose-leaf notebook or a folder to organize your achievement record. Buy plastic sheet covers to keep the pages in good condition.

Do the Work

1. In your achievement record, place copies of certificates, diplomas, letters of recommendation, your Social Security card, and immigration information.
2. Include photos of your achievements and talents. Do you paint houses? Care for children? Decorate cakes? Keep photos that show what you do.
3. You may also want to include an English paper that you are proud of.

As time passes, you will need to update your achievement record, or put new things into it to show new skills and achievements. Always keep your record up-to-date and ready to show.

Present

1. Before using your achievement record in an interview, show it to a teacher or someone else in your support network. Ask for comments and suggestions. Make changes.
2. Your achievement record is an excellent tool for helping you prepare for an interview. Practice talking about each item. Make sure the items are organized in a logical way. Begin and end with items that make a very good impression.
3. Remember that preparing for an interview means practicing your presentation many times until you can do it perfectly. You will have more confidence, and you'll feel less tense and shy.

✂️💻 Technology Extra

Use a computer to design a cover page for your achievement record. You can also use the computer to prepare labels for your photographs.

Getting Help

Getting and Giving Guidance and Support

Work/School
1

Home
2

Community
3

◆ **Vocabulary** Words for offering and asking for help • Words for talking about difficult issues

◆ **Language** Objects of prepositions • Prepositional phrases

◆ **Pronunciation** *of* after a word ending in a consonant • Holding over final consonants

◆ **Culture** Getting professional help

He did this to me!

What would you do if this happened to you?

Last night, Erin and her boyfriend, Mark, had an argument. Later, when he was drinking, he punctured the tire of her car. Now Erin is afraid to tell her mother, who wants her to stop seeing Mark. Erin really doesn't want to do that because usually he is nice and fun to be with. But when he drinks, she knows that he can be abusive and even violent.

Think and Talk

1. What do you see in this picture?
2. Why do you think this happened?
3. How do you think Erin feels?
4. What would you do in this situation?

What's Your Opinion? Should Erin tell her mother about this problem? Explain your reasons.

punctured
see (someone)
yell

Gather Your Thoughts   Everyone needs help sometimes, but choosing how to get it depends on the person and the situation. Ask yourself these questions:

- Who have you asked for advice or help in the past week? In the past month? Is there anyone in your life with whom you can share your problems?
- Do you reach out for help easily, or do you try to solve problems alone?
- What resources—people, agencies, actions, coping strategies—do you use when you have a problem?

What's the Problem?   Erin had reasons for not wanting to talk to her mother about what her boyfriend did. What are some barriers that may stop people from reaching out for help in situations that could be dangerous? Talk with a partner or think about these questions.

Setting Goals   Read the list of goals below. Then write another goal that is important to you. Rank those goals in order from 1 (most important) to 6. Give reasons for your choices.

_____ **a.** identify community resources that deal with physical abuse and substance abuse

_____ **b.** protect myself from physical or mental abuse

_____ **c.** learn how to solve a problem related to substance abuse

_____ **d.** learn how to communicate with friends or family members who need help

_____ **e.** learn how to talk to agencies and other helping resources in English

_____ **f.** another goal: _____

Tally goals for the class. What percentage of people thought that each goal was most important?

Vocabulary

Circle new words. Brainstorm meanings and sample sentences. Take notes. List other words that you want to learn.

agency

barrier

issue

resource

strategy

communicate

cope

abusive/abuse

violent/violence

Remember?

situation

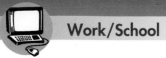
Sharing Your Problems

◆ Get advice from others

◆ Use prepositions correctly

bruise
suspect

Who would you talk to if you had a problem?

◆ **Listening Tip** 🎧 One way to focus your listening is to take notes. Listen to Anna's conversation with her co-workers. As you listen, write two suggestions that her friends give her. The listening script is on page 137.

Idiom Watch!
give up
lose control
pay attention

Anna is talking with her co-workers about her daughter, Erin.

Talk or Write

1. What is Anna's dilemma?
2. What does she suspect about her daughter's boyfriend?
3. What advice do her co-workers give her?
4. Why does Anna share her problem with her co-workers? Would you do that? Why or why not?

What's Your Opinion?   What should Anna do? Why should she do that?

Partner Chat Think about a person with whom you talk often. Who is the person? How often do you talk? When do you usually talk? Where and how do you talk? What do you talk about? What language do you speak?

How often do you speak with your friend?

I speak to her at least once a week.

Write answers to these questions in a diagram like the one below.

Me
I talk with my friend in the evening.

Both of Us
We both speak English with our friends.

My Partner
My partner talks with her cousins back home once a month.

Vocabulary

Circle new words. Brainstorm meanings and sample sentences. Take notes. List other words that you want to learn.

dilemma

protection

confront

ignore

Remember?

suggestion

Grammar Talk: Prepositions and Their Objects

A prepositional phrase is a preposition followed by a noun (and its modifiers) or a pronoun. The noun or the pronoun is the object of the preposition.

Preposition	Noun/Pronoun	Preposition	Noun
during	the break	at	work, home
about	her daughter's boyfriend	before	church
of	them	by	bus, train, car, boat
on	the job	for	years and years
with	my friend	in	Paris, jail

Pronunciation Target • The Word *of*

🎧 *Listen to your teacher or the audio.*

What You See	What You Hear or Say	What You See	What You Hear or Say
Lots of luck!	Lotsa luck!	afraid of him	a fray duh vim
in need of help	in nee duh velp	a friend of mine	a fren duh mine

Talk about the vowel sound you hear in all these examples. What happens with the consonant sound that comes before of?

Activity A Partner Chat Follow-Up Look at the sentences in your Partner Chat diagrams. With your partner, copy the prepositional phrases from your sentences. Underline the noun or pronoun in the phrase. Circle the modifiers. With your class and your teacher, can you make general statements about phrases that have no modifiers?

<u>with (my) friend</u>

Activity B Read the first part of each sentence to your partner. Have your partner complete it with a prepositional phrase.

1. When I feel a lot of stress, I talk _<u>with my friends.</u>_____

2. When my boss yells at me, I complain _____

3. When I feel scared, I talk _____

4. When I need an emergency number, I find it _____

5. When I have a problem, I reach out _____

6. When I don't know what to do, I talk _____

7. When I need to find a doctor, I get a name _____

Activity C In a group of five, get and give advice. Each person chooses a role to play. Use the examples to the right or others that you create.

After the advisors give you their suggestions, leave the group to make a decision. Create your own solution, use a suggestion from one of your advisors, or combine two or more suggestions for a new solution. While you are gone, the rest of the group talks about the best solution to your problem. Return with your decision and compare it to your group's solution.

I would like to know what to do about my noisy neighbor. Her music is driving me crazy.

Friend:
You should call the police.

Counselor:
You should file a report at our town hall.

Boss:
You should confront her first.

Co-worker:
You should ask other neighbors for help.

TASK 1: Start a Resource Guide

Identify people that you can talk to about different kinds of problems. Write your ideas in a chart like this one.

Person	Problem	How to Contact	Notes
my boss	my schedule	go to his office	best time late afternoon
	where to find a good doctor		lives near me and knows the area

Identifying Resources

◆ Practice getting information about important issues

◆ Compare adverb and adjective phrases

Have you ever had problems communicating with someone you love?

alcoholic
rebellious
resentful

◆ **Reading Tip** You don't need to understand every word or sentence to understand a story. Read the story below twice. First, read without stopping. Focus on what the story is about. The second time, underline sentences that you don't understand. Then answer the questions below.

Confronting a Problem

As Anna prepared to talk with Erin, she was nervous. Some previous discussions had turned into upsetting arguments. Anna wanted to encourage her daughter to talk to her. She had read that she must not lose control or tell her daughter what to do. She knew that she had to ask Erin for her opinions. Anna planned to listen more and talk less. She wanted to reassure Erin that she loved her.

But on the day they finally spoke, Anna couldn't control her feelings. She shouted out her worst fears. She ordered Erin to stop seeing Mark immediately. She told her daughter that she was terrified for her. She said that Mark was an alcoholic and an abuser.

Erin had wanted to talk to her mother about the punctured tire, but she became resentful and rebellious. She had planned to tell Anna everything about her problems with Mark. She wanted to tell her that she sometimes felt afraid of him and that she needed help.

However, when her mother got upset, Erin got angry. She accused Anna of being too protective. She shouted at her mother, telling her that she could take care of herself and that she didn't need anybody telling her what to do.

"I *know* what to do!" she screamed as she slammed her bedroom door behind her.

It was then that Anna knew that she needed to find help and began to think about first steps to take.

Talk or Write

1. What was Anna's plan?
2. What happened to the plan when she tried talking to Erin?
3. Erin and Anna both wanted to talk. Why weren't they able to do so?

Class Chat Brainstorm some issues and create a bar graph like this one. Copy it onto the board. Write your name on some sticky notes. Place your name on the graph next to each issue that concerns you. Which issue is most important? Least important? How many people selected each issue?

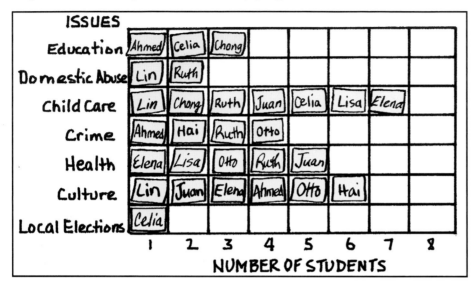

Vocabulary

Circle new words. Brainstorm meanings and sample sentences. Take notes. List other words that you want to learn.

accuse

encourage

reassure

behavior

protective

rebellious

resentful

terrified

Grammar Talk: Adjective and Adverb Prepositional Phrases

Adjective Phrases	Adverb Phrases
Erin's boyfriend is the man **on the right.**	Erin hoped **for a peaceful discussion.**
She is the girl **in the bedroom.**	Anna needs to be patient **with her daughter.**
Erin's car is the one **with a punctured tire.**	They fought endlessly, **without any results.**

The phrases above modify nouns or pronouns. They answer these questions:

***Which** man is Erin's boyfriend?*

***Who** is she?*

***Which** car has the punctured tire?*

The phrases above modify verbs, adjectives, or adverbs. They answer these questions:

***What** did Erin hope for?*

***Who** should Anna be patient with?*

***How** did they fight?*

Pronunciation Target • Holding Over Final Consonants

🎧 *Listen to your teacher or the audio.*

What You See	What You Hear or Say	What You See	What You Hear or Say
How are you?	How war you?	Come on!	Kum mon!
Look out!	Luh kout!	Day or two	dae yor two

With a partner or a group, think about what happens when a consonant sound is followed by a vowel sound. Write a rule for pronouncing these phrases.

Activity A   Think about a time when you wanted to talk honestly and openly, but the other person got upset. Then do one of these things:

- Write a conversation showing what you both said.
- Draw pictures of your conversation. Use speech bubbles to show what you both said. Try to show emotion on the faces.

Try to use some of the words from the vocabulary box on page 44. If you want, share the drawings with your group members.

behavior

domestic

financial compensation

material

slap

victimization

Activity B   Below are two pages from a handbook by a state Office for the Prevention of Domestic Violence. Scan the information. Then answer the questions below.

Resources

State Domestic Violence Hotline
    English 555-6906
    Spanish 555-6908

State Child Abuse and
Maltreatment Reporting Center 555-3720

State Child Abuse
Mandated Reporter's Line 555-1522

Maternal and Child Health Hotline 555-5006

State Council on Alcoholism
and Substance Abuse 555-5353

State Office for the Aging
Senior Citizens Hotline 555-9871

State Office for the Prevention
of Domestic Violence 555-6262

State Crime Victims Board
    Provides financial compensation to crime victims for certain expenses related to their victimization.
    Main Office 555-8727

---

1. Which two organizations would you call if you suspected a neighbor of abusing a child?
2. A friend tells you that her husband slapped her for complaining about his behavior. What organizations could she contact?
3. Which organization could you call for a relative who had a drug problem?
4. You volunteer at a home for older people. You notice that some workers treat the residents rudely. What can you do?

 TASK 2:   Gathering and Using Informational Publications

Look for community, state, or national organizations that provide help with an issue that is important to you. Research their work and share your information with your classmates. Report to the class on one or two organizations that you would especially recommend. For example, you might say this:

"One organization that I have read about is the Child Abuse and Maltreatment Reporting Center. Their number is 800-555-3720. They also provide bilingual assistance. You can ask for someone who speaks your language. You should call them when you suspect that someone you know is abusing a child."

One Step Up
Practice calling a department in your state that deals with the issue that you think is most important. Request a handbook or a pamphlet. With a partner, role-play asking for help.

Substance Abuse: Problems and Solutions

◆ Find information on an organization

◆ Identify topic sentences

hallucinogen

illicit

inhalant

pain reliever

psychotherapeutic

stimulant

tranquilizer

Why do some young people abuse drugs and alcohol?

◆ **Reading Tip** To understand the information presented in tables like these, first read the titles. Next read the vertical ↓ and horizontal ➤ headings. As you read these tables, look for the main ideas that they present.

TABLE A: Alcohol Use in the US in the Year 2000

Percentages by Age Reporting Past Month Alcohol Use, "Binge" Alcohol Use, and Heavy Alcohol Use

AGE	At Least 1 Drink	Binge* Alcohol Use	Heavy** Alcohol Use
12	2.4	1.0	0.1
13	6.7	3.0	0.3
14	11.1	6.0	1.0
15	20.4	12.6	2.5
16	26.4	17.9	4.9
17	32.1	22.9	7.3
18	42.1	30.9	10.3
19	50.0	34.8	13.6
20	55.6	38.5	14.2
21	65.2	45.2	16.7
22	64.1	41.7	13.8
23	62.6	39.8	14.1
24	61.2	38.3	10.4
25	59.0	35.1	9.8
26-29	59.2	33.3	8.9

* Five or more drinks on the same occasion at least once during the month.
** Five or more drinks on the same occasion at least five different days during the month.

TABLE B: Drug Use in the US in the Year 2000

Lifetime, Past Year, and Past Month Use of Illicit Drugs Among Persons Aged 18 to 25

Drug	Lifetime	Past Year	Past Month
Any Illicit Drug	51.2	27.9	15.9
Marijuana and Hashish	45.7	23.7	13.6
Any Illicit Drug Other Than Marijuana	31.9	14.8	5.9
Psychotherapeutic (Nonmedical)+	19.5	9.3	3.6
Hallucinogens	19.3	6.8	1.8
Pain Relievers	14.6	7.3	2.7
Inhalants	12.8	2.4	0.6
Cocaine	10.9	4.4	1.4
Tranquilizers			
Stimulants			
Crack			
Heroin			

+ Nonmedical use of any prescription-type pain reliever, tranquilizer, stimulant, or sedative, but not over-the-counter drugs.

Wow! Mark's not the only 18-year-old with these problems!

Talk or Write

1. What conclusions can you draw from the data in Table A? In Table B?
2. Can you draw more conclusions from the data in the two tables together?

In the US   How to Get Help

In the US, people often get professional help for their problems. There are many low-cost or free programs. An alcoholic may go to a clinic for therapy. A victim of domestic violence may attend a group led by a counselor or psychologist. Sometimes workplace or community programs provide assistance. Schools and religious groups also have programs to help. These programs are usually private and confidential. Professionals can suggest strategies that relatives, friends, or neighbors may not be aware of. The programs can be long-term or short-term, and attendance may be mandatory or voluntary.

☛ Compare Cultures

How do people in your home country deal with these issues? Do they rely on professional help? Do they depend on themselves and their families? What do most people think about these problems? What things are similar to the US? What things are different?

Activity A   As you read the story below, try to understand the meaning of the underlined words by using the context of the story. When you finish, use the context clues to write a short definition for each word in your notebook. Then talk about your definitions with a partner and make changes. Finally, compare your definitions with a dictionary.

Vocabulary

Circle new words. Brainstorm meanings and sample sentences. Take notes. List other words that you want to learn.

- clinic
- counseling
- counselor
- psychologist
- substance abuse
- therapy

- monitor

- confidential
- mandatory
- voluntary

Remember?

long-term/short-term

At the Counselor's Office

When Erin's grades began going down, the high school counselor called her into the office. She told Erin that she was <u>concerned</u> about her grades. She asked if anything in her personal life was having a negative effect on her schoolwork. At first Erin was <u>reluctant</u> to talk about her problem. She <u>insisted</u> that everything was fine. However, she was <u>aware</u> that she needed help, so after a few talks, she decided to tell everything.

The counselor told her that their talks were completely confidential, but she <u>suggested</u> that Anna probably should also be <u>included</u> in the next meeting.

The next day Anna, Erin, and the counselor talked for an hour. The counselor offered a lot of <u>relevant</u> information, including <u>suggestions</u> on how to help Mark with his substance abuse problem. She gave them <u>pamphlets</u> to read and numbers to call. She said that the situation with Mark was <u>unpredictable</u> and could <u>escalate</u> and result in more <u>vandalism</u> or <u>violence</u>. She promised to speak to Mark and his parents immediately and to <u>monitor</u> the <u>situation</u>. She even <u>offered</u> to make some phone calls to legal organizations.

Activity B Below are two paragraphs written by English students. Each has its own main idea, which is stated in the topic sentence at the beginning.

> ○   **Domestic violence is a taboo topic in my country. No one in my country talks about**
> ○   **it. Everybody pretends that it doesn't exist. And so husbands continue to beat their**
> ○   **wives. No one calls it abuse.**

> ○   **I believe that psychotherapy is useless. People pay money to talk to a stranger who doesn't care about**
> ○   **them. Instead, they should talk to caring people—their friends and families. That kind**
> ○   **of counseling doesn't cost anything!**

In your group, brainstorm ideas for five more topic sentences related to the issues in this unit. You can state either an opinion or a fact. Write each idea on a separate strip of paper. Then individually, on a 3 × 5 note card, write three or four sentences supporting the idea of each topic sentence. *Do not copy your topic sentence onto this card.*

Next, as a group, put all your topic sentence strips and paragraph cards into an envelope or a small box. Mix them up and exchange envelopes with another group. Then match the other group's topic sentence strips with their paragraph cards. When you finish, read the topic sentences and paragraphs to the class.

One Step Up

Debate an issue with your group members. In your group, choose sides, or *debate teams,* on the issue. Try to convince the other side that your debate team's ideas are right. Begin your statement by saying, "I strongly agree with . . ." or "I strongly disagree with . . ."

TASK 3: Gather More Information on an Organization

Look at the organizations that you researched in Task 2. List some of the things you would want the agency or organization to do for you. Choose a problem of your own or of someone you know, or a problem shown in one of the charts on page 46. Choose an organization that you think might be able to help you and your classmates solve the problem. Call that organization and ask them to send you more information.

Technology Extra

See if the organization you chose has a web site. Log on to find more information and add it to the list you began in Task 2.

◆ **Reading Tip** Pamphlets and brochures are often easier to read than books or articles. The information often is separated into small sections, and there are photos and art that help make the meaning clear. Now look at this brochure from a community action agency. Read the headings and the introductory paragraphs. Look at the pictures. Then ask yourself what you think you will read about and what you will learn. As you read, underline unfamiliar words or write them in your notebook.

approval

tactful

Idiom Watch!

leave the door open

Action Plans:

How to Fight Domestic Abuse and Substance Abuse

There are several things that you need to do if you want to change an abusive situation. Stop being afraid to talk about your problem. Your conversation should be honest and direct, but always tactful. And no matter how the conversation goes, you need to leave the door open to talk again. Below are some specific and powerful things that you can do.

Fighting Physical or Psychological Abuse in Relationships

First, if you are abusive, get help. If you're not, share your strengths in the following ways:

▶ Accept that abuse affects a whole community. The community pays the price in juvenile crime, drug use, teen pregnancies, higher health care costs, and lost job time and job productivity.

▶ Teach your children that physical abuse and fear are never acceptable in relationships. Then set a good example and practice what you preach.

▶ Find out what services are available in your community. Be ready to refer a victim or an abuser to a place that can help.

▶ Take the problem personally. Your leadership and your involvement are important.

▶ Never say that a friend's or relative's abusive behavior is just due to stress, and never ignore it. Silence can be acceptance, and acceptance is a form of approval. If you don't speak up, the abuser can believe that the behavior is acceptable to you.

▶ Talk honestly with someone you think may be a victim of physical or psychological abuse. Remember that domestic violence could someday threaten the life of your friend or relative. Talking about the situation may not be easy for either of you. The victim may feel embarrassed or guilty. You must be honest but sensitive to her feelings, and you must never judge her. She may not want to talk the first time, but leave the door open by saying something like this:

"I'm worried about you. Are you OK? Do you want to talk about it? It's not your fault and you don't deserve it. I understand, and I won't talk about this to anyone else. I won't tell you what to do. I'll be your friend whatever you decide to do. Did you know there's a number to call to find out more about this? Do you want to call now, or shall I give you the number for later? If not, just remember that I have the number if you ever want to call."

▶ Don't plan a rescue or escape for your friend. And don't criticize her partner, even if you feel he deserves it. You need to try to break through her silence and isolation and be a resource she can use when she wants to.

Fighting Substance Abuse

Get early education on drugs so that you know what you are dealing with. Be able to recognize symptoms of substance abuse. Here are a few of the most common ones, although they can also be signs of other problems:

- ▶ **Physical signs:** repeated health complaints, red and glazed eyes, a lasting cough
- ▶ **Emotional signs:** personality and mood changes, irritability, irresponsible behavior, low self-esteem, poor judgment, depression, and a general lack of interest
- ▶ **Family:** arguing, breaking rules, withdrawing from the family
- ▶ **School:** low interest, negative attitude, lower grades, many absences, discipline problems
- ▶ **Social problems:** loss of interest in home and school activities, problems with the law

If these clues make you think someone you know and care about may have a problem, here's what to do. Find the right kind of intervention, or treatment. Try to match the place, the people, and the services to the person's problems and needs. Here are some guiding rules:

- ▶ Good treatment must consider the many needs of the individual, not just the drug or alcohol use. It must also deal with any possible medical, psychological, social, and learning problems. Substance abuse and mental problems often occur in the same person, so a substance abuse program should offer treatment for other types of problems as well.
- ▶ Medical detoxification is only the first step in substance abuse treatment. Used alone, it almost never gives long-term results for addicts.
- ▶ In good therapy, people learn to build skills to resist substance use and substitute positive actions for drug-using activities.
- ▶ Finally, don't give up! Remember that recovering from substance abuse can be a long-term process. Recovering abusers often need to return to treatment several times. Encourage the former abuser to participate in self-help programs during and after treatment.

Talk or Write

1. Can you think of another tip for helping an abusive person, a victim of abuse, or a substance abuser?
2. What do you think about the tips for helping a victim of abuse? Which of those tips was most surprising to you and why?
3. Many words in this reading were probably new to you. In your group, make a list of the words that any group member didn't understand. Help other group members with meanings that you know. Work together to guess the meanings of words that none of you know. First, look at the context—the rest of the sentence the word is in and the sentences before and after it. If you still can't guess the meaning, look at word parts, especially prefixes.

 Writing Task Imagine that someone you care about is in an abusive relationship—either as a victim or as an abuser—or has a substance abuse problem. Do one of these things to help:

- Write a letter to the person.
- Write a conversation that you could have with that person.

Be as specific as possible with your comments, questions, and advice. Make sure that the advice fits the situation and the possible solutions in your community.

Make a Resource Guide

As a class, create a Resource Guide that lists places to go for help on important issues. You can include government and community agencies and organizations that can help. Also try to find names and phone numbers.

Get Ready

Start by choosing several issues that you find most interesting and important. These can be the same issues you've already discussed in this unit, the issue that you chose for Task 3, or some new issues.

Do the Work

1. State each issue as a question at the top of a page of your guide. Use the form your teacher gives you—one page per issue. For example, you could include these questions:
    - How can I stop my neighbor from blasting her radio after midnight?
    - How can I protect my daughter from her violent boyfriend?
    - How can I get more information about alcohol treatment?
2. On the page, list names of organizations and people that might help with this issue. Also list all phone numbers, addresses, and e-mail addresses. Add notes and additional information.
3. Keep this reference and add to it in the future. Include new resources for new problems.

Present

Choose one issue and report to the class on it. One student reported on this question:

How can I get my landlord to fix the heat in my apartment?

Remember that you don't have to talk about your own issue. You can talk about any issue in this unit or about an issue that is important for a friend or relative.

One Step Up

If possible, publish your class guide on your school's web site.

On Your Own

Making Important Decisions

Work/School   Community   Home
1   2   3

◆ **Vocabulary** Words about small businesses • Words related to safety

◆ **Language** Connecting ideas with *so, because,* and *although* • *who, which,* and *that* in adjective clauses

◆ **Pronunciation** *-tion* ending • Reductions with *have*

◆ **Culture** Independence as a cultural value

> Should I really be trying to start my own business, or would I be safer if I keep working for Sheba?

Would you like to be your own boss?

Donna has always dreamed of opening her own childcare center in her home. Now she has a good chance of succeeding because her friend, Sheba, has offered to be Donna's mentor. Sheba, who is Donna's employer, thinks that Donna is ready to start an independent business. But even with Sheba's encouragement and her own experience, Donna faces a difficult decision.

Think and Talk

1. What do you see?
2. What are Donna and Sheba working on? Why do you think they are working at night?
3. Why do you think that Donna is worried?
4. Think about a good opportunity that you were afraid to take in the past. Describe the opportunity and what you did or what you didn't do.

Vocabulary

decision

encouragement

mentor

opportunity

independent

Idiom Watch!

face a difficult decision

be on your own

Gather Your Thoughts   Choosing between different career paths can be difficult. Sometimes it's helpful to list the good points and bad points of each choice. Talk to a partner about the good and bad points of working for someone else or being independent and starting a new business. Record your ideas on a chart. Here's an example:

Working for Someone Else		Starting a New Business	
Good	Bad	Good	Bad
regular salary	someone else decides your schedule	make your own choices	risk losing everything

What's the Problem?   Not everyone wants to start a business, but at some time almost everyone dreams of changing their life or work. Why is it often difficult for people to decide to make big changes? Talk with a partner or think about this question.

Setting Goals   Read the list of goals below. Then write another goal that is important to you. Rank the goals in order from 1 (most important) to 5.

_____ **a.** decide if I want to be self-employed

_____ **b.** learn some steps to take in starting a small business

_____ **c.** learn to make better decisions

_____ **d.** learn to check my home and workplace for safety

_____ **e.** another goal: _____

Meet with people who made the same number 1 choice. Discuss the reasons for your choice. Calculate what percentage of the class made the same choice that you did. Report back to the class.

Becoming Your Own Boss

◆ Find information to support an opinion

◆ Use *who, which,* and *that* in adjective clauses

businesswoman
fail
inspiring
retire
statistic
workforce

How do you make decisions that are good for you?

◆ **Listening Tip** 🎧 When you listen to something that contains numbers, it's a good strategy to write down the numbers. Listen to this conversation, and write down the number facts that you hear. Listen again if you don't catch everything the first time. Then check your notes with a partner. Tell your partner about the number fact that was most interesting to you. The listening script is on page 137.

Waiting for the children to arrive, Donna and Sheba are watching a television program about starting a business.

Talk or Write

1. What advice did Kim give? Do you agree with her? Why or why not?
2. What did you learn about small businesses? Are they important? Why?
3. Was Sheba correct when she said that 50 percent of businesses succeed? What did Kim say?
4. Look at the numbers that you wrote down. Did any of them surprise you?

What's Your Opinion? Why do you think so many small businesses fail?

Idiom Watch!

catch (something that is said)

Go for it!

write down

Class Chat What percentage of your classmates do you think would like to be self-employed? What percentage prefer to work for someone else? Write a prediction in your notebook. Then survey the people in your group.

Which would you prefer—to work for someone else or to work for yourself? Why?

I'd prefer to work in a job that has security and benefits. My family depends on me.

Divide the number of people who prefer to work for someone else by the number you asked. This gives you the percentage who prefer to work for someone else. Do the same for people who prefer to be self-employed. Graph your answers on a pie chart like this one. Compare your results to your prediction and share your results with the class.

Be self-employed

Work for someone else

Vocabulary

Circle new words. Brainstorm meanings and sample sentences. Take notes. List other words that you want to learn.

benefits

persistence

security

creative

retired

self-employed

temporary

Grammar Talk: Adjective Clauses with *Who, Which,* and *That*

Adjectives	Adjective Clauses
Sheba is an **Ethiopian** woman.	Sheba is a woman **who comes from Ethiopia.**
The Pizza Place is a **successful** business.	The Pizza Place, **which is always busy,** is a successful business.
The **locked** exit door needs repair.	The exit **that is near the kitchen** was locked.

An adjective is a word that describes a noun. An adjective clause is a group of words that does the same thing—describes a noun.

Who refers to people. Which *refers to things.* That *can refer to people or things.* That *and* which *have different uses.* Which *can begin a clause that gives additional but not necessary information. (There is only one Pizza Place.) It begins a clause that has commas around it.* That *begins a clause with necessary information. A clause beginning with* that *doesn't use commas. In the last sentence on the right, we wouldn't know which exit without the* that *clause.* Which *can also be used instead of* that *in a clause that gives identifying information. It could also read, "The exit which is near the kitchen was locked."*

Activity A **Class Chat Follow-Up** Write sentences about your classmates.

Rose said that she preferred to work for a large company because she
wants good benefits.

Activity B With a partner, combine the two sentences in each item below. Use _who, which,_ or _that._ First say the combined sentence, and then write it in your notebook. For some items, there may be more than one correct answer.

1. a. I know a woman.
   b. She started a successful daycare center.
2. a. Ms. Hellman is a teacher.
   b. She also operates a small business in the summer.
3. a. Ethiopia is a country.
   b. It is in East Africa.
4. a. Donna is a woman.
   b. She is afraid to take chances.
5. a. Donna knows about a program.
   b. The program might help her.
6. a. The program makes loans to small businesses.
   b. It is operated by the state.

 TASK 1: Debate an Issue

As a class, debate this issue: It's better to be self-employed than to work for someone else. Divide into small groups of students who agree and disagree with the statement. Follow these steps:

1. **Brainstorm.** Each person should list as many reasons as possible to support his or her argument. Look for ideas in the chart that you made on page 53. Start by saying:
   • It's good to be self-employed because _____.
     OR
   • It's good to work for someone else because _____.
2. **Find information to support your group's opinions.** Look for magazine or newspaper articles, information from web sites or books, facts reported on TV or radio, or true stories about people in business.
3. **Debate.** Meet with a group that supports the other side of the issue. Group members take turns stating their opinions with supporting reasons. Listen to the opinions and reasons of each person on the other side.
4. **Summarize.** When all members of both groups have spoken, one member of each group will summarize their arguments.

One Step Up
Choose one class member from each group to present the debate to another class. Have members of the audience vote on which side presented the best arguments.

Doing the Paperwork

- ◆ Understand how to fill out complex forms
- ◆ Think about independence as a cultural value

caregiver
diagram
draft
facility
fiscal
paperwork
rough

Have you ever completed a difficult form? What was it for?

◆ **Reading Tip** When you complete a difficult application for school, a job, a loan, or a license, follow these steps: Make a photocopy of the form. Read it carefully before starting. Circle new words. Take notes about information that you need to get. Now read Donna's draft of her application form and answer the questions.

Application for Daycare License

This application will not be considered complete until all information has been provided.

Name of Facility: ~~Donna's Angels~~   ~~Happy Children~~   ~~A Place to Grow~~   ~~Donna's Happy Angels Daycare~~

Address: 112 Main Street, Middletown, Ohio   **Phone:** (513) 555-1515

Tax Identification Number: I don't have one! How do I get it?

Name of License Holder: Donna Wright

Address: Same as above

Date facility will begin operation: ?

Facility will be open ~~January~~ September? **to** ~~December~~ June?
              (month)   (month)

Hours of operation are 7:30 a.m. **to** 6:30 p.m. **for** 5 **days per week**

Fiscal Year will be from _____ **to** _____ ?? Help, Sheba!
              (month)   (month)   What is this?

Sheba, my draft is still a little rough. Can you help me with some of the answers?

Please attach the following items.

1. Detailed directions to your facility. OK, I can do that.

2. Diagram of the facility indicating rooms used by children and safety precautions taken. OK, no problem.

3. Daycare workers and family members: Names of all caregivers with their ages, addresses, and phone numbers and all other adults living in the home.   No problem.

4. Name of director of center, resume, and documentation of qualifications. Need resume and diploma

5. Copies of fire and health department approvals. Where do I get those from? How much do they cost???

Talk or Write

1. What information does Donna need before completing the form?
2. During what months will Donna operate her center? During what hours? Why?
3. Will Donna do another draft of this form? How do you know?

Vocabulary

Circle new words. Brainstorm meanings and sample sentences. Take notes. List other words that you want to learn.

cooperation

document

identification

independence

license

operation

precaution

indicate

value

detailed

selfish

Pronunciation Target • *-tion* Ending

🎧 *Circle the vocabulary words that end in* -tion. *What part of speech are these words? Listen to your teacher or the audio. With a partner, mark the stressed syllable of each* -tion *word like this:*

op er A tion

Check a dictionary if you aren't sure. Then read the words to your partner. Together, brainstorm and write other words in the same word families, like this:

identification: identify, identity

In the US   The Value of Independence

Most people in the US believe in the value of *individual* freedom and independence. For example, many Americans value people who make their own decisions more than people who work as part of a group or for someone else. They admire people who overcome barriers and become independent and successful. Sometimes this belief in individual freedom can seem selfish to people from cultures that believe in group action and caring for all people.

☞ Compare Cultures

With your group, talk about what people in your home country and other countries think about the value of independence. Discuss this question: In your home country, do people value independence or cooperation more? Give an example to support your answer. Record your answers in a chart like this one. Report back to the class.

Country	Values Independence More	Values Cooperation More
Poland		✓

Idiom Watch!

do paperwork
run a business

Poland is a country that values cooperation more.

Activity A   On a piece of paper, write the name of someone who you think is a hero. Your hero can be from the US or another country. This person can be real or a character from a story or a myth. Put the papers in a box. Have someone choose one paper and read it. The person whose paper is chosen tells the hero's story to the group. Continue until everyone has had a turn.

One Step Up
Write about the story that was the most interesting to you, but don't write about your own story. What feelings and thoughts did you have when you heard the story?

Activity B   In your group, reread the application form on page 57. The application asks for information and for documents. Make a chart like the one below. In it, categorize what is needed into *documents* and *information.* Donna's notes also show that she knows how to get some of the documents and information and that she will need help with others. On the chart, tell which documents she will get herself and which she will need help with.

Information	Documents
	diploma—get herself

Pronunciation Target • *Could, Should,* and *Would* with *Have*

Written Form
Kim **would have said** where the center was located.
I **could have followed** a sequence.
My plan **should have been** more detailed.

Spoken Form
Kim **wooduv said** where the center was located.
I **kooduv followed** a sequence.
My plan **shooduv been** more detailed.

🎧 *Listen to your teacher or the audio. Can you hear that the word* have *is reduced, or shortened and combined with the word before it? The reduced form of* have *is pronounced like the word* of. *Did you know that English speakers sometimes write* of *instead of* have *by mistake because that's the way they say and hear it?*

TASK 2:   Interview a Small Business Owner

As a class, identify one or two people who know about starting and running a small business. Invite the small business owner (or owners) to class to be interviewed. Then do these things:

- On your own, make a list of questions that you want to ask about running a business.
- Combine your list with the lists of other students. Then choose the best questions and make a typed class list of questions to use in the interview.
- Interview the person.

Why did you choose the type of business that you started?

Did you have a mentor at the beginning? How did that person help you?

Take notes. Record the three most interesting or useful things that you learned from the interview. Compare ideas with your classmates.

Safety First

◆ Be able to check your home and workplace for safety
◆ Connecting ideas with *so, because,* and *although*

decoration
detergent
electrical outlet
fire extinguisher
radiator
vacuum

Have you ever done a safety check on your home?

◆ **Reading Tip** Readings can be easier to understand if you relate the information to your own experience. As you read these health and safety suggestions, think about your own home, a childcare or senior citizen center, or a school that you know about. Think about whether that place is as safe as it can be.

Health and Safety

Here is a list of things to do to make your home safe for children. Even if you don't have children, it's a good idea to check that your home is safe.

Prevent accidental poisoning. Keep all medicines out of reach of children. You must keep cleaning products, detergents, and matches in a place where children can't get them.

Remove any breakable objects that children could reach. Children can swallow or choke on small objects. They may break glass and hurt themselves. If you want to put decorations in your house, look for unbreakable items.

Cover electrical outlets. Look out for loose wires. Small children can trip over wires or pull things over on themselves.

Keep the house clean. Make sure that the children's play area is very clean. Vacuum your rugs every day. Wash all toys often. Be especially careful with toys that children put in their mouths.

Wash your hands often. Always wash your hands before handling food and after using the bathroom.

Cover all heaters, radiators, and pipes to prevent accidental burning. Keep a fire extinguisher nearby. Keep emergency phone numbers near the phone.

Make sure doors can be opened from both sides. You must be able to open every closet door from the inside. You must be able to open bathroom doors from the outside.

Make a diagram of your space. Mark exits and the location of sinks, fire extinguishers, electrical outlets, and heaters. Note safety hazards, and then fix them.

Talk or Write
1. Why do you need to cover radiators?
2. Why do you think closet doors have to open from the inside?
3. What could happen if childcare workers don't wash their hands regularly?

What's Your Opinion? Do you agree with these suggestions? Why or why not?

Group Chat Discuss health and safety rules in other countries with a group. Think about the safety of buildings, food and water, elevators, etc.

Are the rules that keep people safe stricter or less strict in your home country than they are in the US?

I think the rules in Sweden are mostly stricter. Food in restaurants is very safe.

I think that the rules in Kenya are not as strict. Elevators often break down.

Vocabulary

Circle new words. Brainstorm meanings and sample sentences. Take notes. List other words that you want to learn.

- diagram
- hazard
- choke
- repair
- swallow
- breakable
- unbreakable
- loose
- strict

Organize your answers in a chart like this one.

Country	Stricter or Less Strict?	Reason/Examples

Report back to the class. Did people from the same countries always agree?

Grammar Talk: Connecting Ideas with *So*, *Because*, and *Although*

Simple	Combined
Donna washes her hands a lot. The children are healthier.	**Because Donna washes her hands a lot,** the children are healthier.
Donna washes her hands often. Some children get colds.	**Although Donna washes her hands often,** some children get colds.
I vacuum the rug. Children with allergies are more comfortable.	I vacuum the rug, **so children with allergies are more comfortable.**

A complex sentence has one clause that is an independent sentence and one clause that is dependent. Dependent clauses start with words that show relationships, for example, because *or* although. *A compound sentence has two independent clauses joined with a coordinating conjunction that also shows relationships, for example,* so. *Can you identify the dependent and the independent clauses in the combined sentences?*

Activity A **Group Chat Follow-Up** Use your Group Chat chart to write about the health and safety rules in your classmates' countries. Combine sentences using *because*, *so*, or *although*.

The rules in Sweden are stricter, so food in restaurants is safe.

Activity B   In your notebook, combine the pairs of sentences below with *because* or *although*. Use *because* to show cause and effect. Use *although* to show contrast. Then exchange papers with a partner to check your answers.

1. We locked up the cleaning products. Everyone felt safe.

   Everyone felt safe because we locked up the cleaning products.

2. We removed breakable objects. Someone broke a drinking glass.

   Although we removed breakable objects, someone broke a drinking glass.

3. We forgot to put the detergent away. Someone almost swallowed some.

4. Donna provided a detailed diagram. The city gave her a license.

5. We bought a new fire extinguisher. We failed inspection.

6. Sheba washes her hands often. The children are healthy.

Activity C   Make your own safety suggestion list. Brainstorm with your group. Use an idea map like the one below. Think of safety tips that are *not* on the list on page 60. Think about safety tips for each room of a house.

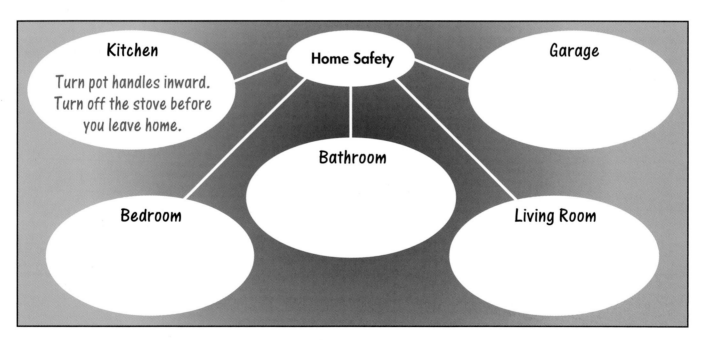

 TASK 3: Safety Check

1. Check your living or work space for hazards. Use the list on page 60 and the health and safety tips that you wrote in Activity C.
2. Answer these questions: Did you find any hazards? What were they? Which was the most serious? Report back to your group.
3. Think about how to fix the hazards. Which ones could you repair yourself? Which ones need professional repair?

One Step Up
List ways to fix the hazards. Try to find out the costs for fixing the problems. Are the more serious hazards the most expensive to fix? Can some simple, inexpensive changes make a big difference?

◆ **Reading Tip**   Before you read, take a few minutes to think about the topic. Write down a few things that you already **know** about small businesses, including things you learned in this unit. Then write down things that you **want** to know about small businesses and the people who run them. After you read, think about the topic again and write down new things that you **learned** from reading the article. You can use a chart like the one on page 64 to record your ideas. This is called a **KWL** chart.

audit

blueprint

Idiom Watch!

Business is slow.

get started

SMALL BUSINESS REPORT

Source: US Small Business Administration

Small businesses are important in keeping the US economy strong, according to a recent *Small Business Profile,* which is a report from the US Small Business Administration. The report shows that small businesses create jobs and new opportunities for many people in or near their homes. Some small businesses are not really small. The definition of a small business is a business that employs fewer than 500 people.

Number of Businesses   In the year 2000 the US had 5,812,100 businesses that employed one person or more. Nearly 99.7 percent of those were small businesses.

Success Rate   About half of all new businesses stay open for four years. The Small Business Administration reports that 66 percent of businesses remain open at least 2 years, 49.6 percent at least 4 years, and 39.5 percent at least 6 years.

Not all businesses close because they are failures. In fact, 57 percent of owners of businesses that closed said that their business was successful at the time it closed. Sometimes, however, business people move, retire, or close one business and open a different one.

Jobs Created   Small businesses create jobs. Almost all companies begin small. They need to grow to stay in business. Small businesses create about two-thirds to three-quarters of new jobs each year. Just over half (50.9 percent) of the nation's employees work in small businesses.

Getting Started   Thousands of people across the US are learning that starting their own business is a good way to take care of family and other responsibilities, have a good income, and get great satisfaction from work. But it's important to remember that starting a small business requires a lot of careful planning and preparation if you want to succeed.

Begin by looking at your reasons for starting your own business and for choosing a particular type of business. Ask yourself hard questions, for example: Do you really want to be independent, or do you want the security of working for someone else? What kind of work are you interested in doing? Do you have the skills you will need for that work?

When you decide what kind of business you want, think about the opportunities and the competition. Will there be customers for that kind of business? Can you do better than your competition?

Finally, create a clear business plan. You will need information on legal and financial requirements. You will also need to give details of what you plan to do and how you expect to keep the business running. The business plan is a kind of map for starting and running your new business.

Running a Home Business   For many people who want to be their own boss, a home business is a good way to start. Careful preparation and a good business plan are still important. Even though you are "at home" every day, you still need to think like a businessperson. Here's some advice on making sure your home business succeeds.

- Act like a businessperson during business hours. Separate your home life and your business life. Rent a post office box and use that address on mail and stationery for your business. Have a phone line in your home just for your business, or use an answering machine for incoming business calls.

- Discipline yourself. Follow a schedule as if you were working for someone else. Unless it's an emergency, do not baby-sit or visit with neighbors during work time.

- Organize your workspace carefully.

- Find a mentor, someone who will answer questions, make suggestions, and help you evaluate ideas. You should also join professional associations.

- Ask your regular customers to suggest new customers.

- Keep accurate records of your expenses. The Internal Revenue Service (IRS) audits home-based businesses more frequently than it audits individuals.

- This is most important: Put some of your earnings into a savings account for times when business may be slow.

Talk or Write

1. In Lesson 1 of this unit you learned that more than 50 percent of small businesses close in the first five years. Do you think that the numbers in this report agree with that success rate? Why or why not?

2. Why might a successful small business close? With a partner, list as many reasons (both negative and positive) as you can for a small business closing.

3. List three or more reasons why small businesses are important to the US economy.

4. Think about a small business that you know. In your opinion, is it successful? Why or why not? Report to the class.

Writing Task Look at the KWL chart you made before starting to read. Think about what you learned from the article. Complete the third column of the chart.

What I **Know** about Small Business	What I **Want to Know** about Small Business	What I **Learned** about Small Business

Use the list in the third column to write a paragraph in your notebook. Give your paragraph this title: "What I Have Learned about Small Businesses."

Look at the second column again. Did you find out what you wanted to know? If you want to learn more, share your questions with your teacher and the class.

Create a Business

Many of us will never run our own small business, but many of us think about it sometimes. What kind of small business would you like to run?

Get Ready

In a group, brainstorm types of businesses that you think might be successful in your area. Ask group members what businesses they think you would be good at. Use those ideas to choose one business that you personally want to run. Then answer these questions about it:

- What business did you choose? What product or service will you provide?
- What skills and experience do you have that are needed for this business?
- Who would be the boss? How many employees would be needed?
- What would be a good location for this business?
- Are there many other businesses of this kind in the area?
- What kinds of people would use this business? Do many of them live close to the business location?
- How can you get more information and help?

Do the Work

Use your answers to the questions above to write about your idea for a small business. Organize the information into three categories:
- description of the business (including why it is a good business for you)
- location and competition
- customers and need for the business

Put the information into three paragraphs. Give your work the title "My Dream Business." Illustrate your work. For example, illustrate the description with pictures of similar businesses.

Present

Present your dream business to your classmates in *one* of these ways:
- Read the description to your classmates.
- Make notes and tell about your business in a one-minute speech.
- Make a poster or bulletin board display.
- Create another kind of presentation. (Suggestions: Make a video, have someone interview you, write a song about your new business, create a computer presentation, etc.)

Think before You Buy!

Becoming an Educated Consumer

Work/School
1

Home
2

Community
3

◆ **Vocabulary** Words that consumers need

◆ **Language** Present and past participles used as adjectives • Embedded questions

◆ **Pronunciation** Stress in compound nouns

◆ **Culture** Technology and progress

Have you ever bought the wrong product?

Bill's camera is broken, and the warranty is expired. When he tried to use his camera this evening, the film wouldn't move. When he took his camera apart to see what the problem was, things got worse. Bill purchased the camera because it seemed like a good deal, but he didn't do the kind of research that educated consumers do.

Think and Talk

1. What do you see in the picture?
2. How do you think Bill feels?
3. Have you ever felt like this?
4. How could Bill prepare before making another purchase?

Gather Your Thoughts

Think about your shopping habits. What kind of consumer are you? How much do you know about a product before you buy it? Do you buy as quickly as possible, or do you search for a product that meets your needs? Use a diagram like the one below to organize your thoughts. In the circle on the left, list all your shopping habits. Then think about good rules for smart shopping and write those in the circle on the right. Finally, write items that are in both circles in the section in the middle.

In your group, compare your smart shopping habits with other people's. Make a group list of smart shopping habits to talk about with your class.

What's the Problem?

What are some reasons that consumers make bad purchases? Are these mistakes always the fault of the consumers? Explain. Think about these questions or talk with a partner.

Setting Goals

Read the list of goals below. Then write another goal that is important to you. Rank the goals in order from 1 (most important) to 5. Give reasons for your choices.

_____ **a.** learn to ask good questions before purchasing an item

_____ **b.** learn to research products in magazines and books and on the Internet

_____ **c.** get information on products from other people

_____ **d.** learn English words for rating different products

_____ **e.** another goal: _____

Tally goals for the class. Talk or write about which ones are most important for your class.

Vocabulary

Circle new words. Brainstorm meanings and sample sentences. Take notes. List other words that you want to learn.

consumer

product

warranty

rate

expired

bargain

purchase

research

Idiom Watch!

a good/bad deal

take apart

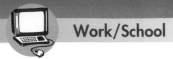

Shopping Smart

◆ Analyze a product you want to buy

◆ Use present and past participles as adjectives

genius

Who do you talk to when making decisions about a purchase?

◆ **Listening Tip** 🎧 If you are listening to a conversation in English and hear an idiom or expression that you don't know, try to think about the meaning of the whole sentence. Sometimes there are clues in the sentence to help you decide what the idiom means. Try this as you listen to a conversation between Bill and his friends at school. The listening script starts on page 137.

Idiom Watch!

come up with (an idea)

figure out

be on a tight budget

Bill is talking with three classmates about the problem with his camera.

Talk or Write

1. What are three things that Bill's classmates tell him to do?
2. What do they think is the best way to learn about new products?
3. What does Bill know about the differences between digital and traditional cameras? Do you know about other differences?

Group Chat   What equipment or materials do you need to fix problems in your home? How do you get advice on the best quality and prices?

What problem do you have?

My smoke detector is broken.

How do you learn about the best quality and prices for smoke detectors?

I usually ask my co-workers or friends for suggestions.

Complete a chart like the one below for people in your group.

Name	Problem	Equipment/ Materials Needed	How Person Learns
Toni	Her smoke detector is broken.	new smoke detector	co-workers, friends

Vocabulary

Circle new words. Brainstorm meanings and sample sentences. Take notes. List other words that you want to learn.

budget

equipment

explanation

feature

digital

high/low quality

technical

traditional

return

Grammar Talk: Present and Past Participles Used as Adjectives

Read the sentences in each column. Notice the two endings, -ed and -ing, on the words in bold type.

The camera instructions were **confusing** Bill.	The **confusing** instructions did not help him.
Bill had **assembled** the pieces of the camera.	Some of the **assembled** pieces were broken.

The words that end in -ing are present participles. The words that end in -ed are past participles. In the sentences in the left column, can you see that these words show action? The present and past participles are parts of the verbs in those sentences. In the sentences in the right column, the same words are used to describe objects. In those sentences, the participles are used as adjectives to describe nouns or pronouns.

The past participles of most irregular verbs also are irregular. Those forms do not end in -ed, and they must be memorized. For example, the verbs choose, buy, *and* sell *are irregular. Can you say or write the past participles of those three verbs? Can you list other irregular past participles with your class and your teacher?*

Activity A   In your notebook, write sentences using the present or past participles of six of these verbs as adjectives:

break	buy	purchase	return	speak
budget	choose	research	sell	write

When you finish, check your sentences with a partner. Have you used the participles correctly?

Activity B   **Group Chat Follow-Up** In your notebook, write sentences about at least two problems you discussed in your Group Chat. In the second sentence about each problem, use a participle as an adjective.

Toni needs to buy a smoke detector. Her old one is broken.

I can't always answer my phone. I need an answering machine.

Activity C   Write about the tasks for which you use machines or equipment at home. Write your tasks in Column A of a chart like the one below. Then use participles as adjectives to tell more about each task in Column B.

A	B
I iron my clothes.	I use my <u>ironing</u> board. I hang the <u>ironed</u> clothes in the closet.

 TASK 1:   Do an Informal Product Analysis

Think about one product that you want to buy. Gather information about the product from classmates, co-workers, friends, and a local store. Record the weaknesses *(cons)* and strengths *(pros)* in a chart like the one below. Bill created this chart after gathering information about digital cameras.

Product: Digital Camera	
Weaknesses	**Strengths**
printed photos may be poor quality	some cameras record sound and make videos
too much time spent uploading to Internet	can share photos easily with others on e-mail
difficult to get printed photos	can review photos instantly and delete poor ones

Doing the Research

◆ Practice doing research to make good purchasing decisions

◆ Recognize and respond to embedded questions

| fair |
| overall |

How can you find out about a product that you want to buy?

◆ **Reading Tip** Before reading a table or chart, look at the title. Then look at the headings for the columns and rows and other words in darker print. Now find this information in the table below. Can you predict from these words what information this chart will give you?

Go To: http://

Overall Ratings *In Performance Order*

Models	S-speed	M-task C-800	E-mini MS 3	D-smart S400
Price	$800	$900	$450	$375
Overall Score	E	VG	G	F
Weight (oz.)	14	18	35	8
Multi-function	E	G	G	F
Mega-pixels	3.3	2.3	2.1	2.1
Print Quality	G	F	F	P
Comments	Can take still photos and video clips.	Has optimum exposure in low light.	Has automatic "red-eye" reduction.	Includes modem, no need for PC to use on Internet.

Talk or Write

1. Which model of camera is the most expensive?
2. What do you think the letters next to the headings *Overall Score, Multifunction,* and *Print Quality* mean?
3. What can you conclude from the ratings chart?
4. Which camera would you choose? Why?

What's Your Opinion? Think of a product that you want to purchase. What four features would you want rated in a chart for that product?

Class Chat Ask questions using the chart below. If someone answers "Yes," write the name next to that item. Continue until you have a name for every item.

Have you learned how to shop on the Internet?

Vocabulary

Circle new words. Brainstorm meanings and sample sentences. Take notes. List other words that you want to learn.

model

performance

rating

score

source

technology

Find someone who . . .

• has learned how to shop on the Internet.	
• knows where to find bargains on appliances or technology.	
• finds out how much products should cost before buying.	
• knows which stores offer the best prices on technology.	
• knows where to find information comparing different products.	
• reads product ratings.	
• knows how to find consumer information sites on the Internet.	

Grammar Talk: Embedded Questions

Will you tell me **who broke the camera?**	Do you know **when this item will go on sale?**
Can you show me **how you do it?**	Do you know **how long this is going to take?**

Embedded *means "included inside of." Notice the embedded questions in dark type inside the longer questions above. In the first sentence, the word order is the same as in other* who *questions. What happens to the word order in the other three sentences?*

Pronunciation Target • Stress in Compound Nouns and Common Phrases

🎧 *Listen to your teacher or the audio.*

classmates   **day**dreams   **camera** store   **picture** frame

What happens with stress in a compound noun or commonly used phrase? Did you notice that the stress always falls on (or in) the first word?

Activity A   In your notebook, embed these questions in other questions. Check the word order in your sentences carefully. Then read your sentences to a partner.

1. How much does this camera cost? *Do you know how much this camera costs?*

2. Which one is better? *Can you figure out* ?

3. Where is the expiration date?

4. Where did you find it?

5. Why is it so expensive?

6. Where can I find it?

Activity B   **Class Chat Follow-Up** Write sentences using the information from your Class Chat chart. Then write a question about each sentence using words and phrases like these: *Can you tell me . . . ? Do you know . . . ? Did you figure out . . . ?* When you finish, ask the class one or more of your questions. Remember that more than one answer may be possible.

Mohamed has learned to shop on the Internet.

Can you tell me who has learned to shop on the Internet?

 TASK 2:   Research and Rate a Product

Alone or with a partner, rate a product that you need or want to purchase—food, over-the-counter medicine, a technology product, and so on. First, look for information about the product. If there are similar brands of the same product (such as a refrigerator or a frozen pizza) or companies that offer the same service (such as two airline companies), choose two or three and compare their features, price, and quality. Use the information and questions below as a guide for your research. After doing the research, would you still buy the product? Why or why not?

Sources of Information
- consumer product magazines (in library)
- specialized magazines for products, such as car magazines (in library)
- advertisements and product information sheets
- recommendations from friends
- conversations with sales clerks
- web sites

Questions to Answer
- What is the name of your product?
- Where can you purchase it?
- What is the price range for your product?
- What kind of warranty does it provide, if any?
- What did you learn that surprised you?

⌨️ Technology Extra

Using the information from your research, make a table on the computer similar to those in consumer guides.

Consumer Rights and Consumer Awareness

◆ Read and analyze a section from a textbook

◆ Learn about US attitudes toward science and technology

defective

reliability

nonprofit

violate

Do you know what rights you have as a consumer?

◆ **Reading Tip** In English you often can predict the meaning of science or social studies words because they look like words in other languages. Read this article on the consumer movement in the US. List new words that look like words in a language that you know. Guess their meanings.

Help for Consumers

Many organizations in the US protect consumers. In 1962, President John Kennedy began the consumer-protection movement. Kennedy said that a consumer had four basic rights—to have safe products, be informed, choose, and be heard. In 1973, the federal government set up the Consumer Product Safety Commission. The CPSC researches all new products for quality, safety, and reliability.

Today nonprofit consumer organizations across the US deal with consumer affairs. They inform consumers about products and provide tips. They also help consumers get payment for damaged or defective products or for injuries caused by their use. The Better Business Bureau, or BBB, encourages fair business practices, helps consumers whose rights have been violated, and provides reliability reports about companies. These reports usually tell whether the company is a member of the BBB and if it has had any consumer-related problems. News reports also warn people about illegal business practices and problems with products.

Unfortunately, some businesses will not stop unfair practices just because new laws make them illegal. The best way for consumers to protect themselves is to become educated. People need to be careful of fraud. They need to be especially careful about buying over the Internet or the phone. They need to take the time to research the product they want to buy and the business they want to buy it from. These practices can save hours of time, money, and worry.

I really want to know more about protecting my rights as a consumer.

Talk or Write

1. Name two important events in the history of US consumer rights.
2. What does the word "movement" mean in this reading?
3. Give examples of fair and unfair business practices.

In the US   Technology and Progress

Many Americans believe in the power of science and technology to create a better future for themselves and their children. Americans think less about history and tradition than people from other cultures do. They believe that they have control over the future, that change produces improvements, and that most new things and ways are better than old ones. Having the newest technology is a way of "keeping up with the times," an important goal for most Americans. Advertising often encourages people to buy new models of machines that they already have. Many Americans depend heavily on technology in their everyday lives, and for this reason, many consumer ratings are done for technology products.

☛ Compare Cultures

Are there government organizations that help consumers in your home country? How do people find out about which products to buy and where—especially technology products? Complete a diagram like the one below to compare and contrast your country and the US.

Attitudes toward Science, Technology, and the Future

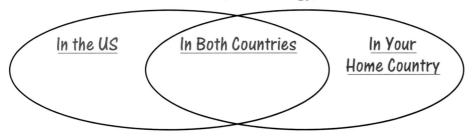

In the US   In Both Countries   In Your Home Country

Activity A   In what ways has technology changed what we buy and how we shop today? In groups, create present/past pairs of sentences by comparing how consumers shopped in the first half of the 20th century with how they shop today. Have one person in each group write the comparisons. Stop after five minutes and report your results.

In the past, people bought more fresh food.

Today most food is processed and packaged.

Vocabulary

Circle new words. Brainstorm meanings and sample sentences. Take notes. List other words that you want to learn.

- fraud
- improvement
- practice

- inform
- warn

- damaged
- fair
- illegal

Idiom Watch!

keep up with the times

Remember?

depend on

One Step Up

Take another five minutes to think of how each comparison your group made could change again in the future.

Activity B   Your teacher will divide the class into two equal groups, Group A and Group B. Each group will support one of these opinions:

A. Technology makes it easier to be an informed consumer.

B. Technology makes it more difficult for consumers to choose well.

In your group, prepare to support your opinions with good examples from the US and other countries that you know. Your teacher will tell you how much time you have. At the end of that time, each group will present its opinions to the other group. After both groups present, discuss the ideas as a class, vote, and take a class survey on the issue.

Activity C   In a group, do a taste test of three different brands of a food product. Each group has three samples—for example, three brands of peanut butter. Each person uses a clean plastic spoon to taste each brand. Describe differences you taste. Which sample tastes the best? Create a class list or chart with the result. Tally how many students would buy each brand.

 TASK 3: Create an Original Product Ad

With a partner, follow these steps to create an ad for a product:

convincing
dramatic
slogan
supplies

1. Choose something that you would like to sell to your classmates.
2. Gather as much information about it as you can.
3. Brainstorm slogans often used in ads. This list can help you:
   - last chance to buy
   - the best deal
   - the greatest offer
   - while supplies last
   - a great opportunity
   - our lowest prices ever
   - only in our store
   - new and improved
4. Complete an idea map with the most important or interesting information and the best slogans that you gathered. Use these phrases and sentences in your product ad.
5. Make an advertising poster using your phrases and slogans with pictures of the product.
6. Convince your classmates to buy your product by presenting your poster. Read your ad or role-play it. Make the presentation funny, serious, or dramatic, but make it as convincing as possible. Students can rate the ads by telling which products they would or wouldn't buy and why.

◆ **Reading Tip**   One way to better understand what you read is to first skim it quickly. Then read again slowly, reading word groups—phrases and clauses, or even whole sentences. It's easier to understand when you read this way. Try it with this reading.

Let the Buyer Beware

This advice is provided by the Federal Citizen Information Center. The FCIC can help you find information about federal government agencies, services, and programs. It tells you which office can help with problems. The FCIC does not handle consumer complaints, but it helps consumers send complaints directly to companies and agencies through its web site.

complaint

extended

headquarters

legitimate

policy

toll-free

If you take these steps before making a large purchase, you have a good chance of avoiding problems and being happy with what you bought:

- Decide exactly what you want, need, and can afford.
- Research the product or service using information from the Federal Citizen Information Center in Pueblo, Colorado. The FCIC's toll-free number is 1-888-878-3256, and its web site is www.pueblo.gsa.gov.
- Ask family and friends to share experiences and give recommendations.
- Compare prices. Get several price estimates.
- Learn about and compare warranties. Some warranties are required by law. Call a state or local consumer protection office to find out more.
- Research a company's complaint record with your local consumer affairs office and the Better Business Bureau. Find out how many and what kinds of complaints have been filed. For a large purchase, look at the complaint files to see what the company did about the complaints.
- Read and understand any contract that anyone asks you to sign. Are all the blanks filled in? Are any promises included in writing?
- Extended warranties or service contracts help businesses make extra money. Someone may talk to you about these as you are paying. Think in advance if not having to worry about problems is worth the price.
- Check out a seller's return policy and get it in writing.
- Consider paying by credit card. If you later have a legitimate complaint against the seller, you may not have to pay a charge on your credit card.

To make a complaint about a business, use these tips:

- It's usually best to contact the business that sold you the product or performed the service. Most companies want to keep you as a customer.
- Many stores also have a toll-free number. If you can't find it, dial toll-free directory assistance at 1-800-555-1212. Contact the headquarters of the company or manufacturer by phone or the Internet. Ask for the consumer affairs office. Describe the problem calmly. Tell in as few

words as possible the action you would like the company to take. Ask for the name of the person that you talk to. Take notes on the date, what the person said, what you said, and the next steps you agree on.

- If this doesn't work, write a letter stating what happened. Describe the problem, what you have done to resolve it, and the solution you want (for example, your money returned or the product repaired or exchanged). Include a copy of the receipt, the date of purchase, the name and address of the store where you purchased, and information about the warranty. Do not send original documents, only copies. Send your complaint by first-class certified mail to be sure it reaches the person.
- After you call or write, give the person time to resolve your problem. Save copies of *all* letters to and from the company.
- If the company won't help, contact a local, state, or federal agency to tell you your rights and investigate or resolve an issue. Try the Better Business Bureau or the Consumers' Union for help.
- If your case still is not resolved, you can take legal action. Small Claims Court will usually resolve cases quickly and inexpensively, and you won't have to hire or pay a lawyer. Small Claims Court deals with cases in which the amount of money is limited. The maximum amount varies from state to state. It may be between $2,000 and $5,000.

certified mail

investigate

receipt

resolve

Talk or Write

1. Which new words could you understand when you read in word groups?
2. What was still difficult to understand? What other clues do you need?
3. With a partner, list all participles used as adjectives in this reading and write their meanings.

Writing Task

In an idea map, brainstorm answers to these questions about a time when you purchased a product that you were not happy with in either the US or your home country. Then write a one-paragraph story about your experience.

- What did you buy?
- What was wrong with it?
- What did you do or say to complain?
- What happened as a result?
- What would you do differently now that you have read the article above?

Create a Class Consumer Guide

With your class, create a consumer guide for some or all of the products that you looked at in the following tasks in this unit:
- Task 1, Do an Informal Product Analysis, page 70
- Task 2, Research and Rate a Product, page 73
- Task 3, Create an Original Product Ad, page 76

Get Ready

Choose the products that you will review. Use the checklist that your teacher gives you. Each student should present at least one product review. Plan a page with these features for each product:
- name of product at the top of the page
- general information about the product
- rating charts for each product from the Internet or consumer magazines
- short summary of information at the bottom of each page

Do the Work

1. For each product that you include, gather or create the information that you need.
2. Divide the guide into sections like these: Food Products, Technology, Services, Home Appliances. Decide where each product should go.
3. Number your pages. At the beginning of the guide, add a contents page. List the page numbers of the sections and the products in each section.
4. Add a resource page at the end of your guide. List all your research resources there—names of web sites, magazines, books, and so on.
5. Ask for comments and suggestions from your teacher. Make changes if necessary.
6. Design a cover for your class consumer guide. You can include photos, drawings, or symbols of products. You may want to make a collage cover using pictures and words cut from magazines.

Present

As a class, present your guide to another class in your school or program. Put your guide in a school or program library so that other students can look at it closely.

✎💻 Technology Extra

If some students know how to work with computer graphics and type, let them suggest how to make a cover design on the computer.

Protecting Your Rights

Understanding Your Rights

Home
1

Work/School
2

Community
3

◆ **Vocabulary** Legal terms

◆ **Language** Adverbs of time with the past perfect • Special problems with prepositions, articles, gerunds, and infinitives

◆ **Pronunciation** Consonant blends

◆ **Culture** Written and verbal contracts

But we said that we wanted a sunroof and four-wheel drive.

Has a salesperson ever tried to cheat you?

Last week Mr. and Mrs. Wu put a $500 deposit on a contract to buy their dream car. Today, when they go to pick up the car, they discover that it doesn't have the features that they wanted. They ask for their $500 deposit, but the dealer refuses. He tries to pressure them into taking the car anyway. The Wus refuse. They leave disappointed and angry, without their deposit or the car.

Think and Talk

1. What do you see in the picture? What's the problem?
2. Has anything like this ever happened to you or to someone you know?
3. What should the Wus do next? What advice would you give them?
4. How important do you think it is to get a contract in writing?

What's Your Opinion? The car dealer said that he was keeping the deposit because he had to pay for delivery. Was it right for him to keep the deposit? Explain.

dealer

dream car

four-wheel drive

sunroof

Gather Your Thoughts

What should people in situations like this do? Brainstorm answers to this question with your group. Make an idea map like the one below.

How can people protect themselves from being cheated?

What's the Problem?

Are immigrant families cheated in the US more often than people who were born here? Explain. Talk with a partner or think about the question.

Setting Goals

Read the list of goals below. Then write another goal that is important to you. Rank the goals in order from 1 (most important) to 6. Give reasons for your choices.

_____ **a.** learn how I can protect my rights

_____ **b.** learn about the language in contracts

_____ **c.** learn the meanings of some legal words

_____ **d.** learn what to do or say in a courtroom

_____ **e.** learn how to read legal documents

_____ **f.** another goal: _____

Tally goals for the class. Talk or write about which ones are most important for your class.

Vocabulary

Circle new words. Brainstorm meanings and sample sentences. Take notes. List other words that you want to learn.

    contract

    deposit

    rights

    cheat

    pressure

    protect

    refuse

    disappointed

    legal

immigrant

Read the Fine Print!

◆ Understand how a contract protects your rights
◆ Use adverbs of time with the past perfect

Have you ever signed a contract you didn't understand?

◆ **Reading Tip** Before you read the whole contract, look at the text in bold type.

> acknowledge
> authorized
> in accordance with
> terms and conditions

SALES CONTRACT

BUYER'S NAME: _Kuang Shang Wu/ Mamie Wu_
ADDRESS: _36 Bush Street_
RESIDENCE PHONE: _415-555-9683_
MAKE: _____ MODEL: _____
COLOR: EXTERIOR _hunter green_ INTERIOR _gray_

SALESMAN: _Jamie_
CITY: _San Francisco_ ST: _CA_ ZIP: _94115_
BUSINESS PHONE: _____
BODY TYPE: _minivan_
VIN # _2B4GH2538PR125932_

I acknowledge that by my signature on this Contract, I have read its terms and conditions and have received a true copy of this contract.

BUYER: _Mr. Kuang Shang Wu_ DATE: _1/13/04_
ACCEPTED BY: _M. S_____ DATE: _1/13/04_
                MANAGER

Doesn't "4WD" mean four-wheel drive?

CASH DELIVERY:

24 pkg
AUTOMATIC TRANS
4WD
3.0 1 MPI V-6 Engine
AIR CONDITIONING
SUNROOF
MOLDINGS
DUAL HORNS
STORAGE DRAWERS
7 PASSENGER SEATING
SUNSCREEN GLASS

TAXABLE TOTAL:	$16,560.00
SALES TAX: _8.25%_	1,366.20
TOTAL CASH PRICE DELIVERED:	17,926.20
LESS DEPOSIT SUBMITTED WITH ORDER:	-500.00
CASH DUE ON DELIVERY:	$17,426.20

I agree that this Contract includes all of the terms and conditions **AND THAT THIS CONTRACT SHALL NOT BECOME BINDING UNTIL ACCEPTED BY YOUR AUTHORIZED MANAGER.** A deposit is requested with all contracts for factory-ordered vehicles. I acknowledge that by my signature on this Contract, I have read its terms and conditions and have received a true copy of this Contract.

IF THE NEW MOTOR VEHICLE HAS NOT BEEN DELIVERED IN ACCORDANCE WITH THIS CONTRACT WITHIN 30 DAYS FOLLOWING THE ESTIMATED DELIVERY DATE, THE CONSUMER HAS THE RIGHT TO CANCEL THE CONTRACT AND TO RECEIVE A FULL REFUND.

Talk or Write

1. What features are listed as included in the car?
2. What information in this contract do you think is most important?

Remember?

consumer

Group Chat With a partner, choose two questions to ask five other pairs. Partner A asks the questions. Partner B records the answers on a chart.

Have you ever signed a contract in this country?

Yes, I have.

Vocabulary

Circle new words. Brainstorm meanings and sample sentences. Take notes. List other words that you want to learn.

agreement

obligation

refund

binding

Write your question at the top of your chart.

1. Have you ever signed a contract?
2. Have you ever asked for legal advice?
3. Have you ever been pressured into buying something?
4. Have you ever asked for a refund?
5. Has a salesperson ever cheated you because of your English?

Name	Have you ever _signed a contract_ in this country?	Had you ever _signed a contract_ in your home country?
Jolie	Yes, I have.	No, I hadn't.

Idiom Watch!

the fine print

Grammar Talk: Adverbs of Time with the Past Perfect

Main Clause with Past Perfect Verb	Dependent Clause with Adverb of Time
She **had read** the contract	**before** she signed it.
He **had taken** her to court	**when** she refused to pay.
They **had accused** the dealer	**after** he cheated them.
I **hadn't gone** to court	**until** I saw that there was no other way.

Before reading further, review with your teacher the meaning of "main clause" and "dependent clause."

Read each main clause in the left column and the dependent clause in the right column. What happened first in each pair of clauses, the action in the left column or the action in the right column?

Look at the dependent clauses in the right column. What wh- question do all the adverbs (in bold type) answer? What tense is used in the dependent clause when the verb in the main clause is in past perfect tense?

Remember that either clause can be first in these sentences. Now read each sentence aloud, but this time put the dependent clause before the main clause. What punctuation mark would you add after the dependent clause if you wrote these new sentences?

Activity A   Group Chat Follow-Up Work with your partner. In your notebook, write sentences with the answers from the Class Chat chart.

Jolie has signed a contract in this country, but she hadn't signed a
contract in her home country before coming here.

Activity B   Play Concentration with your group. On a set of 3 × 5 cards, write these clauses, each clause on a separate card:

- I had decided to take an English class . . .
- I had planned to write you a note . . .
- I hadn't thought about our agreement . . .
- He took her to court . . .

- . . . before I came to the US.
- . . . when I had the time.
- . . . until you asked me to pay.
- . . . after she refused to pay the bill.

Using these cards as models, each person should make another set of eight cards with his or her own clauses. The first clause in each sentence should have a past perfect verb. The second clause should begin with an adverb of time and have a past tense verb.

Put all the cards together, mix them up, and put them on a table with the words down. The first player turns over any two cards. If they make a logical, realistic sentence, the player keeps them and turns over two more. If they do not make a logical sentence, the next player takes a turn. The game ends when all cards are matched. The person with the most cards win.

If someone doesn't think that a sentence is logical, that person explains why. The player who made the match explains why it is logical. The group can discuss and vote to decide whether the player should keep the cards.

Activity C   Do you have a class contract? Think about these questions, and brainstorm answers in your group.
- What does your teacher expect from you as a student?
- What do you expect from your teacher?
- What obligations do you and your teacher have to the school?

 TASK 1:   Make a Class List of Legal Terms

Follow these steps to make a class list of legal terms (words or expressions that have a legal meaning). You can use the list as a reference during the rest of this unit. Be sure to leave room for more terms.

1. Reread the contract on page 82. Pay special attention to the small print.
2. Make a list of the *legal terms,* or words and expressions that have a legal meaning. Talk about their meanings in your group. If no one in your group knows a word, find it in a dictionary.
3. Work together with your teacher to make the class list of legal terms.
4. Make a wall chart of the terms and their meanings.

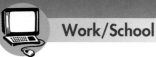

Taking Legal Action

◆ Learn how to take legal action

◆ Understand verbal and written contracts

When could Small Claims Court work for you?

◆ **Listening Tip** 🎧 Understanding recorded messages is not easy. Try these things:
  • Take notes.
  • Go slowly. Stay relaxed. The recording is usually on 24 hours a day.
  • Replay the message. Listen as many times as you need to.
  • Talk to someone. Listen for instructions on how to reach a live operator.
  • Ask a friend for help if you can't understand the message.

Listen to this message twice before answering the questions below. The listening script is on page 138.

case
claim
court
fee
judge
pound (#) key
replay
Touch-Tone phone

During the morning coffee break at work, Mrs. Wu is calling Small Claims Court for information.

Talk or Write

1. What three things should Mrs. Wu do if she wants to take the car dealer to Small Claims Court?

2. What would you do in the same situation?

What's Your Opinion? Is it a good idea to go to Small Claims Court?

Pronunciation Target • Initial Consonant Blends

 Listen to your teacher or the audio.

Claim, **Cl**ass
Pray, **Pr**ide, **Pr**oduct
Plaintiff, **Pl**an, **Pl**ease
Property, **Pr**essure
Small
Speak, **Sp**end, **Sp**ring
Stay, **St**are, **St**ate
Try

How many syllables do you hear in the words small, speak, *and*
state? *Notice that initial consonant blends that begin with the letter* s
in English are never pronounced as two syllables. For example, the
word stay *has only one syllable. It is not pronounced* "es-tay."

Vocabulary

Circle new words. Brainstorm meanings and sample sentences. Take notes. List other words that you want to learn. These words are all legal terms. Add them to the list of legal terms that you started in Task 1.

claim

court

defendant

dispute

evidence

file

judge

plaintiff

property

sue

support

witness

Activity A With a partner, write more words that begin with consonant blends. Create sentences with the words from the Pronunciation Target and the words you listed. Use as many words as you can in each sentence. Read your sentences to your partner.

1. _Stop staring at the strange student._

2. _____

3. _____

4. _____

Idiom Watch!

to be up to
(someone)

📼💻 Technology Extra

On a cassette recorder, record yourself and your teacher reading the sentences that you wrote for Activity A. Then listen and compare your pronunciation with your teacher's. Talk about the differences.

Activity B Alone or with a partner, read the listening tips on page 85 again. Have you ever tried any of these things? Which ideas are new for you? What other advice do you have for listening to recorded phone messages? Write another idea of your own. Report back to the class.

In the US   Written and Verbal Contracts

Mr. and Mrs. Wu had a written contract with the car dealer. Informal verbal agreements between friends are common when small amounts of money are involved. However, in the US a formal written contract is expected if the amount of money is large or if people don't know each other well. People in the US use contracts often and expect them in many situations.

☛ **Compare Cultures**

In your home country, do people often make agreements without written contracts? When do people use written contracts? Work with a group of learners from your home country or culture. Talk with your teacher and your class about differences between the way people use contracts in the US and the way they use them in your home countries.

Activity C   Ask group members to tell about any court cases that they have seen or participated in. Choose one case and answer these questions:
- Who was the plaintiff?
- What was the dispute about?
- What evidence did the plaintiff present to support the case?
- What evidence did the defendant present?
- What was the decision? Did you agree with it?

In a group, present the case to the class. Explain clearly what happened.

One Step Up

In a group, take the roles of judge, plaintiff, defendant, and witnesses. Role-play the Wus' Small Claims Court case or the case that your group presented in Activity C.

Technology Extra

Students who have a VCR or a DVD recorder can record a TV show with a court scene. Watch the show in class. As you watch, stop the recording frequently to review legal terms used by the characters. Add any new terms to the list that you started in Task 1.

 TASK 2:   Listen to a Recorded Message

Listen to a recorded phone message. You and a partner call the same number and listen to the message. You could call the Small Claims Court number, another government service number, the 800 number of an airline, a movie theater for its schedule, etc. Take notes and compare. Report back to the class. Use the questions below as a guide for your report.
- Did both of you get the same message?
- Did you understand most of the message?
- How many times did you have to replay it?
- What parts were difficult to understand?

Speaking Up for Your Rights

◆ Learn more about your rights and what happens in court

◆ Use problem prepositions, articles, gerunds, and infinitives

What would you do if you had to speak up for your rights?

Idiom Watch!

speak up (for)

◆ **Reading Tip** In the reading below, Mr. Wu describes his day in court. As you read, picture in your mind what is happening.

Our Day in Court

We'll never forget our day in court. We were so nervous. We were afraid that I would forget to tell the judge all the important details. I was really worried that the judge would not understand me. My accent gets stronger when I'm nervous. Sometimes I have to repeat things that I say.

Even though we had prepared our speech together, we were still anxious. We had all our notes with us. We even put numbers on the cards to remember what to say first. We wrote some difficult words that we wanted to use in the court. And we underlined the most important sentence: "We demanded our deposit back, but the dealer refused to return it." We kept repeating that sentence many times until we knew that we could say it clearly in court.

The judge was very patient with us. She didn't ask many questions. Probably that was because the dealer did not come to court. I guess he knew that he was wrong.

We showed the judge the contract and explained how the dealer had not delivered the car described in the contract. We didn't have to repeat any of our sentences. The judge understood everything that we had said. The judge made a decision in our favor. She even increased the amount from $500 to $535.

We received a check in the mail a few weeks later. Now we know that we can speak up for our rights in this country. We could do this again if we had to. However, we hope that we'll never meet another dealer who tries to cheat us!

From this experience we've learned the value of a contract. We also learned that it's good to be persistent. We're proud that we were able to speak up and protect our rights.

Your Honor, I demanded my deposit back, but he refused to return it.

Talk or Write

1. Why did the Wus feel nervous? How did they control their feelings?

2. How do the Wus feel about defending their rights in the future?

Class Chat   Find out from your classmates what kind of rights they are most interested in knowing about. Ask 10 people in your classroom one of the questions listed below. Record your answers in a chart like the one below. Write your question at the top of your chart.

Are you interested in knowing more about

- your rights as a parent?
- your right to privacy?
- your rights as an immigrant?
- your rights as a tenant?
- your rights as a worker?

- your rights as a consumer?
- your children's rights?
- your rights as a US citizen?
- your rights as a landlord?
- another topic?

What kind of rights do you want to know more about?

Name	Answer

Vocabulary

hearing

demand

settle

anxious

patient

persistent

Grammar Talk: Choosing and Using Difficult Language Forms

The following language forms are especially difficult for students of English. Review them by studying the examples carefully.

Choosing and Using Prepositions of Time: *On, In,* **and** *At*

You are scheduled to appear in court **on June 21, 2002.**

Your hearing is **at 3 P.M.**

The judge's decision will be mailed to you **in February.**

The prepositions in, on, *and* at *are very exact for each time expression.*
So, if you need to use a month you must say or write the preposition in.
If you say or write a complete or specific date, use on.

Choosing and Using Articles: *A/An, The,* **and No Article**

Nonspecific
- You need to sign **an** agreement.
- You need to fill out **a** form.

General
- People go to court to settle disputes.

Specific
- You can get a form at **the** courthouse.

Choosing and Using Gerunds and Infinitives

Used as a noun (gerund)
- **Winning** this case is important to Mr. Wu.
- **Suing** the dealer is the only way to get his money back.

Following a verb (infinitive)
- Mr. Wu wants **to win** the case.
- He will have **to sue** the dealer.

A *and* an *should be used with* **unknown** *and* **nonspecific** *target words.*

If you use a verb in a noun form, add -ing.

Activity A You are Partner A or Partner B. Cover your partner's side of the exercise. Dictate, or read, the sentences printed in red to your partner. Then listen to your partner's dictation. Fill in the blanks.

Partner A

1. Mr. Wu's case was heard on January 4.

2. He arrived _____ 3 P.M., exactly on time.

3. In February he'll get his money back.

4. _____ the day he gets his money back, he'll be very happy.

5. Winning his case in court made him very proud.

6. He wanted _____ the dealer from cheating other people.

Partner B

1. His case was heard _____ January 4.

2. He arrived at 3 P.M., exactly on time.

3. _____ February he'll get his money back.

4. On the day he gets his money back, he'll be very happy.

5. _____ his case in court made him very proud.

6. He wanted to stop the dealer from cheating other people.

Activity B Look at your Class Chat responses. Form a group with three people. Discuss your rights. Use the idea map below as a model. Present your map to your class. Your classmates have the right to disagree with you. As a group, defend your point of view.

Rights as a Parent

I have the right to

teach my child how to behave

educate my child in my culture

protect my child from physical danger

speak to my child's teacher

have my child tested for learning disabilities

 TASK 3: Present Your Argument

Think of a problem in your own life or the life of someone you know that could be settled in Small Claims Court. Describe the problem and the arguments that would be made during the court hearing:

• arguments used by you
• arguments used by the defendant
• the defendant's response to your arguments
• your response to the defendant's arguments

◆ **Reading Tip** Before you read, look over the entire guide. Skim over some of the questions to get an idea of what the guide covers. Then read the guide carefully, looking for the main ideas.

Have you ever bought a technology product that needed repair after its warranty expired? Did you know that many manufacturers and stores offer to fix your product if you purchase a service contract when you purchase the product? Here is some information to remember the next time you need to decide whether to buy a service contract. As you read this guide, think about whether a service contract could have been useful to you in the past.

Service Contracts and Extended Warranties

To Purchase or Not to Purchase?

Q. *What is a service contract?*

A. A service contract is a kind of repair insurance, sometimes called an "extended warranty" or a "service agreement," that you buy separately from the product.

Q. *How is a service contract different from a warranty?*

A. Essentially, a warranty is not bought separately. It comes with the product you purchase.

Q. *Are there different kinds of service contracts?*

A. Yes, there can be many different kinds of service contracts. For example, a service contract may require you to pay a certain amount for repair service. Or it may require you to pay labor or transportation charges.

Q. *Are you saying that a service contract may not pay for repair service when I need it?*

A. It may not pay for everything. For example:
- It may pay for labor only or parts only.
- It may not pay for every part.
- It may limit the number of repairs.
- You may have to pay a certain amount for each service call.
- It may not pay for in-home service.

Q. *What are some pros and cons of service contracts?*

A. Service contracts may help you pay for expensive repairs and routine maintenance. On the other hand, be sure the service you receive is given by technicians who are trained to work on your product brand and who will use appropriate replacement parts.

Q. *How can I make sure that the service contract I buy with a new product does not duplicate the warranty or overlap it?*

A. Read the warranty to find out how long the warranty lasts and what it covers. Your new electronic product warranty may cover most repair costs, sometimes for 90 days, sometimes for a year or more.

Q. *My VCR needs maintenance service to keep the heads clean. Can a service contract help pay the cost?*

A. Yes, some service contracts do cover routine maintenance.

Q. *How can I decide whether to buy a service contract?*

A. Read the warranty, read the service contract, and compare. Weigh the cost of the service contract against maintenance and repair bills you may have later. If you cannot first read the service contract, do not buy it! Make sure all the blank lines are completed.

Q. *Who sells service contracts?*

A. The retailer who offers you a service contract may be selling it for the dealer, the manufacturer, or a separate service company. Ask the salesperson for time to study the contract. Also ask if the retailer sells more than one kind of service contract. If so, compare them.

Q. *What happens if my service contract company goes out of business?*

A. Unfortunately, there is little you can do if this happens. The best way to protect yourself is to make sure before purchase that the company is reputable and has insurance so you can get a refund.

Talk or Write

1. What are some of the main points of this guide?
2. Did you learn any new words? What are the most important terms to remember?
3. Which questions do you feel are most important?
4. Which information surprised you?

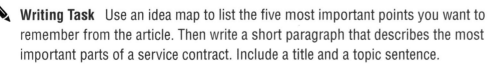

Writing Task Use an idea map to list the five most important points you want to remember from the article. Then write a short paragraph that describes the most important parts of a service contract. Include a title and a topic sentence.

Create a Personal Legal Glossary

A glossary is a mini-dictionary of words used for a specific purpose. Develop a glossary of legal terms.

Get Ready

Look at the list of legal terms you started in Task 1 and any new legal words from Lessons 2 and 3. Brainstorm other words that would be useful to people in legal situations.

Do the Work

1. Create a legal glossary by alphabetizing your word list and adding definitions. Check the dictionary for exact meanings.
2. Type your list on a computer, or have a group member who has good handwriting write it.
3. Add other useful information. For example, what are the rules for court conduct in your area? Check the Small Claims Court or the Internet. Call Small Claims Court in your area for a brochure, or ask someone in the group who knows someone who has been to court.
4. Have group members watch a court TV program and report back to the group their observations on courtroom procedures and vocabulary.

Present

Present your project in a way that you enjoy.
- Give your glossary a title and simple cover. Publish it for students in another class.

OR
- Make copies of your list for people from other countries who need to know more about the US legal system.

OR
- Dramatize your courtroom knowledge:
  - Brainstorm to choose an issue.
  - Assign roles: plaintiff, defendant, judge, witnesses, and other roles.
  - Plan a simple court scene and practice it in your group.
  - Present the case to classmates.
    Note: The judge can decide who wins the case, or you can ask classmates to vote on the winner.

Participating in Your Community

Becoming an Active Community Participant

Work/School 1   Home 2   Community 3

◆ **Vocabulary** Language for participating in a democracy

◆ **Language** Present and past participles used as adjectives • Past participles of irregular verbs

◆ **Pronunciation** Disappearing /h/ of function words

◆ **Culture** Tradition of self-reliance and community involvement

What do you like and not like about voting in your home country or in the US?

Galina, a new citizen, is voting for the first time. She becomes anxious when she sees proposals on the ballot. She selects her candidates, but she doesn't know how to react to the proposals. People are waiting, so she makes a quick choice and leaves, feeling that she has wasted her vote.

Think and Talk

1. Where is Galina? What do you see in the picture?
2. What happened? Why do you think Galina felt she wasted her vote?
3. Has anything like this happened to you or to anyone you know? Explain.
4. How should people prepare to vote?

What's Your Opinion? If you are not sure about a candidate or an issue, should you vote anyway? Why or why not?

> candidate
>
> waste

Gather Your Thoughts   Galina wanted to vote to be an involved and active US citizen. In what ways can people participate in a democracy? What does a responsible citizen need to know and do? Make an idea map like this one to organize your thoughts:

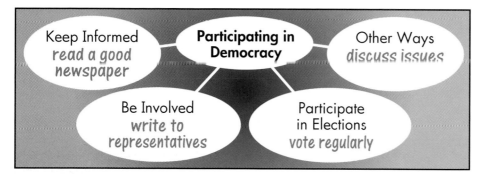

What's the Problem?   What are some of the barriers to being an informed voter? What are some obstacles to being actively involved at the local, state, or national level? Talk with a partner or think about these questions.

Setting Goals Read the list of goals below. Then write another goal that is important to you. Rank the items in order from 1 (most important) to 6. Give reasons for your choices.

_____ **a.** learn more about local, state, and national issues

_____ **b.** learn how to become more active in my community

_____ **c.** learn about the role of a responsible citizen

_____ **d.** learn the language necessary to keep informed

_____ **e.** learn how to communicate with my representatives at all
levels of government

_____ **f.** another goal: _____

Tally goals for the class. What percentage of people thought that each goal was most important?

Vocabulary

Circle new words. Brainstorm meanings and sample sentences. Take notes. List other words that you want to learn.

ballot

booth

election

proposal

representative

senator

participate

waste

active

informed

involved

responsible

Remember?

issue

Participating in Elections

◆ Discuss voting procedures

◆ Use present and past participles as adjectives

> excited/exciting
>
> league
>
> record

What should you do before you vote?

◆ **Reading Tip**   Thinking about what you know about a topic can help you understand new information. As you read this article about a first-time voter, think about what you already know about voting.

Interview with a Conscientious First-Time Voter

Galina Gagarin

Max Flax, reporter

I visited Galina Gagarin, a proud new voter, at her school on Election Day. Ms. Gagarin agreed to this interview as part of our series on new citizens. I asked her about her first voting experience in the US. She said that she had gotten up very early and that she had been very excited.

Was the experience as exciting as you expected? "Yes, it was. But voting is also a little intimidating. I needed time just to figure out how to mark the ballot."

What happened then? "Well, I took a deep breath and voted. At least I *hope* I did. I hope my vote was correctly recorded. I was too embarrassed to ask for help."

Did you know who to vote for? "The candidates for mayor were all good, but I knew which one I wanted. That's because we had talked about all the candidates in my English class. However, part of the ballot was confusing to me. I should have read it before I voted. I wish that I had learned more about the proposals."

How could you have done that? "A teacher at my school told me that ballots are sometimes printed in the newspaper. Or you can contact your political party headquarters for information. The League of Woman Voters is great too. The League helps men and women learn more about the issues, and it presents issues objectively. Next time, I'm going to be ready to make an informed decision."

You are continuing with your English classes even though you are already a citizen? "Yes. I think that it's important to continue my education. I want to learn more about the United States."

So what do you still want to learn? "I am fascinated by the US political process. I know I still have a lot to learn to be a fully informed voter."

Do you believe that one person's vote can make a difference? "Oh, yes, I do. That's what's so great about this country. I am interested in good schools. Next time I will vote for a candidate who has a record of supporting them. I am also concerned about good, affordable childcare. I'm going to watch the new mayor's voting record on that very closely. This citizen is going to pay attention to the issues from now on!"

Talk or Write

1. The headline describes Galina as a conscientious voter. Do you agree? Why or why not?
2. Was her first voting experience positive, negative, or both? Why?
3. What words tell you that Galina's voting experience was stressful?
4. What had she done to prepare to vote? What else could she have done?

Idiom Watch!

concerned about

figure out

make a difference

record a vote

take a deep breath

voting record

Class Chat Talk about your voting experience in the US or in your home country. How did you feel? What surprised you about the process? Record your answers in a chart like the one below.

Name	When did you vote?	How did you feel?	What was surprising?
Andrew	a year before I came to the US	excited	the large number of voters
Anna	a few months after I became a US citizen	intimidated	other parties on the ballot

Vocabulary

Circle new words. Brainstorm meanings and sample sentences. Take notes. List other words that you want to learn.

candidate

district

affordable

conscientious

democratic

embarrassed/embarrassing

fascinated/fascinating

intimidated/intimidating

Grammar Talk: Present and Past Participles as Adjectives

Notice that the verbs in the sentences on the left are all "verbs of emotion." See how they change when they are turned into adjectives.

Galina was **excited** by the elections.	The elections were **exciting** to Galina.
She was **confused** by the proposal on the ballot.	The proposal on the ballot was **confusing.**

*The past participle of a verb (verb + -ed or irregular form) and the present participle (verb + -ing) can be used as adjectives. The past participle tells how someone feels: "I am **fascinated** by the American political process."* Fascinated *says how I feel about the American political process. "The American political process is **fascinating** to me." The present participle,* fascinating, *describes something that will make someone feel fascinated.*

What happens to the verb when the subject of the sentence experiences the emotion? What happens to the verb when the subject does not experience the emotion?

Activity A **Class Chat Follow-Up** With a partner, take turns reading sentences. Partner A reads sentence 1. Partner B makes a new sentence, changing the past participle (*-ed*) to the present participle (*-ing*). Then Partner B reads sentence 2, and Partner A changes the sentence.

1. Galina was embarrassed by her lack of knowledge.

   Galina's lack of knowledge was embarrassing to her.

2. José is very interested in the democratic process.
3. People were confused by the ballot.
4. Galina is fascinated by politics.

Activity B Look at the information on this voter registration card. Why did Galina receive this card in the mail? Talk about why she needs the card.

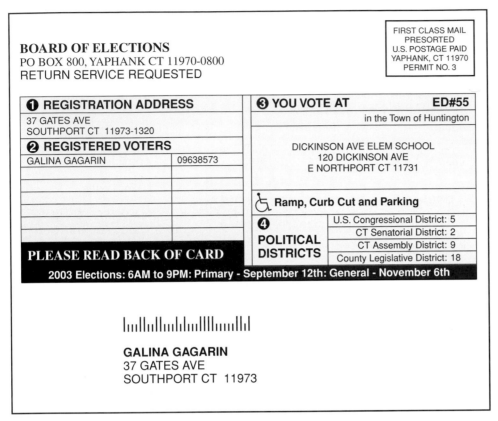

① REGISTRATION ADDRESS		❸ YOU VOTE AT	ED#55

BOARD OF ELECTIONS
PO BOX 800, YAPHANK CT 11970-0800
RETURN SERVICE REQUESTED

FIRST CLASS MAIL
PRESORTED
U.S. POSTAGE PAID
YAPHANK, CT 11970
PERMIT NO. 3

❶ REGISTRATION ADDRESS
37 GATES AVE
SOUTHPORT CT 11973-1320

❷ REGISTERED VOTERS
GALINA GAGARIN   09638573

PLEASE READ BACK OF CARD

❸ YOU VOTE AT   ED#55
in the Town of Huntington

DICKINSON AVE ELEM SCHOOL
120 DICKINSON AVE
E NORTHPORT CT 11731

Ramp, Curb Cut and Parking

❹ POLITICAL DISTRICTS

U.S. Congressional District:	5
CT Senatorial District:	2
CT Assembly District:	9
County Legislative District:	18

2003 Elections: 6AM to 9PM: Primary - September 12th: General - November 6th

GALINA GAGARIN
37 GATES AVE
SOUTHPORT CT 11973

Activity C   Do you believe that one vote can make a difference? If you do, stand with the *Yes* group. If you don't, stand with the *No* group. With your group, prepare an argument to convince the other group to join you. Select two people from your group to speak. After everyone has spoken, people who change their opinion can move to the other group.

YES: Politicians look closely at numbers. Every vote helps persuade a politician to take a certain position.

NO: So many people vote that a single voter can't change an election.

 TASK 1: Registering to Vote

Your teacher will give you a blank voter registration form. Fill it out with your own information. If it requires information that you don't know, such as the voting district in which you live, brainstorm ways to find out that information with your class. If you are not a US citizen, you cannot vote in federal elections, and you probably can't vote in state or local elections. But you can communicate your concerns to elected officials.

Keeping Informed

◆ Identify basic responsibilities of government

◆ Use the past participle of irregular verbs

What community issues are important to you and your family?

◆ **Reading Tip** When you read a complex form, think about what information you expect to find. As you look at this ballot, ask yourself what features you expect.

> charter
>
> commission/
> commissioner
>
> erasure
>
> void

OFFICIAL BALLOT FOR THE GENERAL ELECTIONS

Foster County Town of Southport	2003 General Election Col. 1	2003 General Election Col. 2	2003 General Election Col. 3
Instructions	**MAYOR**	**POLICE COMMISSIONER**	**PROPOSALS**

Instructions

1. Mark in blue or black pen or pencil.
2. To vote for a candidate whose name is printed on the ballot, completely fill in the circle beside the name of the candidate.
3. To vote for a candidate whose name is not printed on the ballot, print the name and fill in the circle in the blank space following the candidate for each public office.
4. Any other mark or writing, or any erasure made on the ballot outside the voting circles, will void this entire ballot.

MAYOR

Mark SIEGEL ○
Fernando GARCIA ○
Kathryn COLON ○
_____ ○

POLICE COMMISSIONER

Stephen FLAXMAN ○
Norman STRINGER ○
Betsy F. STRINGER ○
_____ ○

PROPOSALS

Shall the Town Charter be amended to make the Children's Services Agency an independent town agency to provide for the care and protection of children?

| YES | ○ |
| NO | ○ |

Shall the Town Charter be amended to make the Office of Immigrant Affairs a town agency to assist immigrants and protect immigrants' rights to Town services?

| YES | ○ |
| NO | ○ |

Talk or Write

1. Which sections of this ballot are most difficult to understand? Why?
2. From reading this ballot, what did you learn about what a proposal is?
3. Are the instructions for casting a vote clear on this ballot?

What's Your Opinion? Is it important to have an agency to protect children? To assist immigrants?

Idiom Watch!

cast a vote

public office

Group Chat Talk together about the ways that you keep informed about issues or events in your community, state, or nation. What other resources do you plan to use?

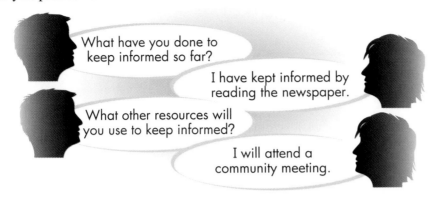

What have you done to keep informed so far?

I have kept informed by reading the newspaper.

What other resources will you use to keep informed?

I will attend a community meeting.

Complete a chart like the one below with your group.

Name	Your Past Resources	Your Future Resources
Galina	I have read political magazines.	I will attend more town meetings.

Grammar Talk: Past Participle of Irregular Verbs
Look at the past participles of irregular verbs in these sentences.

One of the voting machines was **broken.**

Have you **heard** about the new agency to help immigrants?

Galina hadn't **read** the proposals before she went to the polling place.

Our teacher had **done** a lot of research before she voted.

The candidate for mayor was **known** in her district.

Can you identify the structures in which past participles are used? What is the main verb for each of these past participles? Brainstorm a list of other common irregular verbs and their past participles.

Activity A With a partner, discuss some actions you have taken in the past to become more active in your community and involved with issues. Write in your notebook about what you both have done.

Me: I have written to my representative.

My partner: She has spoken to a member of the League of Women Voters.

Both of us: We have taken citizenship classes.

Neither of us: We haven't attended any community meetings.

Activity B   How much do you and your group members know about your state? Find out which group in your class is able to answer the most questions correctly:

One Step Up
Write one or more questions for other groups to answer.

1. What is the capital of your state?
2. Name several cities in your state.
3. Name some important mountains, lakes, or rivers in your state.
4. Who is your governor?
5. Who is one of your senators in Washington?
6. Who is one of the representatives for your area in Washington?
7. Who represents you in your state legislature?
8. When did your state become a state?
9. What is your state flower?
10. What is your state bird?

✌🖳 Technology Extra

If no one in your group knows an answer, find it on the Internet.
Locate a state government web site.

Activity C   National, state, and local governments have different responsibilities. The responsibilities of national and state government are defined by the US Constitution. Each state government defines the responsibilities of the local governments in that state. It may define several forms of local governments, such as city and county governments. With your group, decide which responsibilities are carried out by local, state, and federal government. Review the answers with your teacher.

> declare war
>
> disability insurance
>
> unemployment
>
> worker's compensation

local government responsibility _____   1. To make traffic and parking rules

_____   2. To set up laws for international trade

federal government responsibility _____   3. To regulate business between states

_____   4. To provide for the health and welfare of the citizens

state government responsibility _____   5. To make laws about unemployment, disability insurance, and worker's compensation

_____   6. To regulate garbage disposal

_____   7. To provide schools

_____   8. To declare war

_____   9. To make regulations for construction of buildings

TASK 2:   Stay Informed

Invite a local representative to your program. With your group, prepare for the meeting. Make a list of questions for your representative about any issue that concerns you. Practice asking these questions and be ready to take notes.

Getting Involved

◆ Learn how to be a more active community member

◆ Learn about the activities of community agencies and organizations

coincidence
exaggerated
opposition
struggle
tolerance

Have you ever attended a community meeting? If you have, why did you attend? If you haven't, why not?

◆ **Listening Tip** 🎧 To understand a discussion, it helps to have background information. Read the caption below for background information before listening to this discussion. The listening script starts on page 138.

Galina has been reading and hearing a lot about the town's plan to build a new low-income housing project not too far from the local high school. Now she is at a community meeting. A representative of the town council is answering people's questions about the project.

Talk or Write

1. What was the main issue discussed at the meeting?
2. What concerns did people voice? What responses did the speaker offer?
3. Which answers surprised you?
4. What other questions would you ask?

In the US Self-Reliance and Involvement Traditions

Rather than wait for the government to solve problems, people in the US sometimes start grassroots organizations. Your community center's after-school program was probably started because a group of parents wanted activities for their children. Some local organizations develop into national movements. Such organizations address issues like health problems, environmental damage, hunger, and housing shortages. Many groups work for political action. A grassroots organization somewhere in the US is working on almost every community concern.

Vocabulary

Circle new words. Brainstorm meanings and sample sentences. Take notes. List other words that you want to learn.

housing project

shortage

town council

grassroots

low-income

overcrowded/overcrowding

☛ Compare Cultures

How are community problems resolved in your home country? What kind of grassroots organizations exist there? How are they similar to or different from grassroots organizations in the US? Have any groups grown into national or international movements?

Pronunciation Target • The Disappearing *h*

🎧 *Listen to your teacher pronounce these words in two ways, stressed and unstressed. Can you hear the difference?*

he her him   ee er im

Now, listen to your teacher pronounce each word in a phrase.

What organization **did he** join?
I've **seen her** at the polling place.
Have you **heard him** at the meeting?

Did you notice that the phrase sounds like one word? Say these sentences with a partner. Notice the position of your tongue and lips. Sometimes when the h *is at the beginning of a word, it disappears and you hear only the vowel sound.*

Activity A   Ask a partner these questions. The answer to each question must start with *h*. Listen carefully to the way your partner pronounces the answer. Then switch roles. Decide which answers have a disappearing *h* sound.

1. If it's not *her,* it's who? It's _____.
2. If it's not *him,* it's who? It's _____.
3. If you're not *there,* you're where? You're _____.
4. Where do you live? I live at _____.
5. What verb do you need for the present perfect tense? I need the verb _____.
6. In what city are many movies made? Movies are made in _____.
7. If it's not soft and easy, it's what? It's _____.
8. If it's very, very big, what is it? It's _____.

Activity B Are you active in your community? Do you want to be? Think about ways in which you have been able to make a difference. And think about things you wanted to do but couldn't or didn't. For example, have you ever helped people in your neighborhood? Did you volunteer your services with a community organization? Have you ever been a member of a neighborhood committee? Talk to a partner about your participation in your community.

Have you ever helped out your neighbor?

Yes, I've done some shopping for the elderly lady next door.

Have you wanted to do more for your neighborhood?

I've always wanted to organize a Neighborhood Watch group, but I don't know where to start.

Activity C With your class, identify some local issues that are important to you and your community. List the issues on the board. Decide which issue is most important to you. Work in a group with others who chose the same issue. Brainstorm specific concerns and questions about this issue. Make an idea map like the one below.

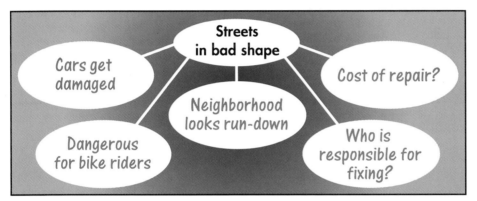

Streets in bad shape

Cars get damaged

Cost of repair?

Neighborhood looks run-down

Dangerous for bike riders

Who is responsible for fixing?

If your group put questions on the map, decide how you could get answers. List possible sources of information and answers below your map.

TASK 3: Write about an Issue

In your group, work with the idea map from Activity C. Brainstorm possible solutions to the problem. Try to get answers to your questions and use that information in your discussion. Add the solutions to the map. Present your issue to another group. As you talk about your concerns, ask other groups for their ideas. List their concerns and solutions. Then in your group, write a letter to the editor of your local newspaper about the issue. Identify the concerns, and present one or more possible solutions.

One Step Up
Stay involved. Send the letter you wrote in Task 3 to your local government representative or to the government agency that is responsible for that issue. If possible, you may want to send the letter as an e-mail message.

◆ **Reading Tip** Relating an article or story that you read to your past experiences can help you understand it better. Before you read this newspaper story, think of your own feelings about becoming a citizen.

Why I Became an American Citizen

By Christine Castro

When my mother became a US citizen in 1980, I asked her why her hair wasn't blond. I was 5 at the time. I don't remember it, but my mom tells me when she walked through the door after her swearing-in ceremony I just stared at her, puzzled.

I thought being American was having blond hair, eating at McDonald's, and watching fireworks on the Fourth of July. I thought being American must be the greatest thing in the world. I wanted to be an American.

Instead, I was a Filipino girl with brown skin, choppy black hair, and slanted eyes. Nobody looked at me and knew that I had been in this country since I was 9 months old. In grade school, children ran circles around me chiming, "ching, chang, chong," as if I were a strange foreigner. When I spoke to them in clear English, they were often startled.

My parents worked hard, paid their taxes, and abided by the laws. We held green cards. We had every right to be here. But when I traveled outside the country or applied for a job, I had to flash my green card. When I turned 18, I couldn't vote like my friends. I spoke English, pledged allegiance to the flag, and lived here, but I still wasn't American.

My mom wanted to come here as a young woman to study architecture at a graduate school. But she was the only girl in the family, and moving to another country at that time was unheard of. When she finally moved here, she says, she decided to take advantage of the privileges of citizenship. After all, this would be her home.

Had my dad, Tomás, become a citizen as well, my brothers and I would automatically have become naturalized. But he was not ready. There was martial law in the Philippines, and relinquishing his Filipino citizenship meant giving up his property rights. Besides, he said, he wanted the decision to be our own.

At last, my father, brother Ricky, and I applied for citizenship together in December, interviewed in April, and took our oaths in late June. My dad says it was the growing anti-immigrant sentiment that finally persuaded him to apply. Ricky wanted to be able to vote and travel easily. I couldn't wait for the day when I wouldn't have to show the green card to prove I belonged.

I kept telling myself I shouldn't be nervous, but I couldn't help it. I feared that though I had lived here my entire life, they would decide that

abided
advantages
allegiance
mesmerized
privileges
puzzled
swearing-in ceremony

they didn't want me. And I was also frustrated. I knew that so many Americans did not know the answers to some of the questions I would be asked at my interview. And I didn't think it was fair that I could be discriminated against for that. But I passed the test and survived the interview.

From then on, I eagerly awaited my swearing-in ceremony invitation, circling the mailbox like a vulture. And when I did get the letter, I counted the days, telling everyone the big day was near. I'm not sure what I expected—a wave of inspiration to overcome me as I pronounced my oath, to walk out of that convention hall mesmerized. I would like to say when 4,000 people waved their plastic flags and the national anthem resounded, I was in awe. I want to say, "Yes, I am proud to be an American."

But I'd be lying if that was the only side of the story. My 10-year-old cousin in the Philippines wrote me and said she didn't understand why I became a US citizen. "Aren't you proud to be a Filipina?" she asked. The truth is, I'm proud to be both. I am still a Filipina, holding dearly the values and traditions with which I was raised. But I am now an American. I will do what I can to help this country as it has helped me. It is my duty as a citizen.

My naturalization certificate is tucked in a manila folder in a bookshelf in my dad's office. To me, it is just a piece of paper with my name and picture on it. It is what the certificate stands for that is very dear to me. I can say that I am an American. I do belong.

Talk or Write

1. What is the writer's main idea about becoming an American citizen?
2. What arguments does the writer use to prove her point?
3. What examples does she provide to make her point?
4. How are the writer's experiences similar to yours? How are they different?

Writing Task

Write a paragraph on one of these topics:
- why I want to become a US citizen
- why I do not want to become a US citizen
- why I became a US citizen

Make a Community Resource Guide

It's helpful to have the names, addresses, and phone numbers of your local, state, and national officials, as well as agencies and organizations that deal with issues that concern you. To keep that information available, make a community resource guide.

Get Ready

You will need

- a list of your local, state, and national government officials
- a list of agencies or organizations that you are interested in
- materials to make your guide: lined paper for the pages, card stock or colored paper for the cover, and clips or rings to hold the pages together

Do the Work

1. Group the names of the officials into three categories: local, state, and national. Start a new page for each category. Put information about agencies and organizations in a separate category.
2. Prepare an entry for each official. Write the person's name, job, address, phone number(s), and e-mail address. Next to each name, write the type of issues that the official could help you with. Do the same for agencies and organizations.
3. Prepare a cover for your guide. Put a title and your name on it.
4. Put together the cover and the pages of your guide with rings or removable clips (so that you can add new information and update information if necessary, particularly after an election).

Present

1. Show your guide to your teacher or someone else in your classroom. Ask for comments and suggestions. Make changes.
2. Share your information, including addresses and phone numbers, with other members of your class. Explain why you selected the agencies and organizations that you included.
3. Take notes, and include additional resources and contacts that other students who completed their presentations gave you.

One Step Up

Include any available web site addresses for the listings in your guide.

✂️🖥️ Technology Extra

Type your information on a computer. Use special features, such as bold type, to make it easier to read. Print the pages for your guide. Save the file so you can make changes.

It's Never Too Late

Finding Your Learning Style

Community
1

Work/School
2

Home
3

◆ **Vocabulary** Words for giving a speech • Words about ways to learn

◆ **Language** Past continuous • Past perfect continuous

◆ **Pronunciation** Disappearing sounds and syllables

◆ **Culture** Learning at any age

Have you ever had to speak English in front of many people? How did you feel?

Willie's daughter is getting married. She and her parents are talking with a wedding planner. Willie's wife and daughter are excited, but he is worried. Willie came to the US from Poland 23 years ago. He has worked hard, and he owns a successful business. But he doesn't understand everything the wedding planner says, even when he checks his dictionary. She doesn't always understand him either. Willie wants to give a speech at the wedding. He wants to express his pride. But he thinks that his English may embarrass his family.

Think and Talk

1. What do you see in the picture? How do you think each person feels?
2. What's Willie's problem? Do you know anyone who had a similar problem? What did that person do?
3. If a friend asked you how to improve his or her English, what advice would you give?

Gather Your Thoughts   Willie has been planning to improve his English for a long time, but he hasn't taken the first step for many reasons. With a partner, brainstorm a list of the feelings and thoughts—both positive and negative—that people may have before starting something new. Make an idea map like this one to show the thoughts and feelings:

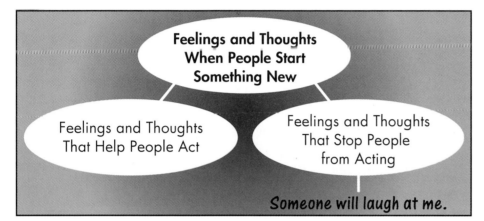

Feelings and Thoughts When People Start Something New

Feelings and Thoughts That Help People Act

Feelings and Thoughts That Stop People from Acting

Someone will laugh at me.

What's the Problem?   Look at the negative feelings and thoughts you listed under the circle on the right. Have some of these feelings and thoughts ever stopped you from taking an important step in your life? Why?

Setting Goals   Read the list of goals below. Then write another goal that is important to you. Rank the goals in order from 1 (most important) to 6. Give reasons for your choices.

_____ **a.** learn ways to study better

_____ **b.** find out about the different ways, or styles, that people have of learning

_____ **c.** find out about my personal learning style

_____ **d.** use my personal learning style to learn better

_____ **e.** learn about different approaches to learning

_____ **f.** another goal: _____

Tally goals for the class. Talk or write about which goals are most important for your class.

What Works Best for You?

◆ Learn how to find educational resources
◆ Use the past continuous tense

certified

credit/noncredit

trial

Do you know how you learn best?

◆ **Reading Tip**   When you look in the yellow pages, do these things: Read slowly. Look for important details. For example, look for location, hours, and specific services. Take notes or highlight interesting listings. Now read this page from the phone book where Willie found information about English classes. Take notes on the ads that look good. Read critically. Do any schools look too good to be true? Why?

Language Schools   317

▶ **Language Schools**

AAA School
Workplace English.
Our graduates get jobs.
Dunmore......................555-3653

ABBY LANGUAGE CENTERS
*ENGLISH and
12 Other Languages*
• We Teach Online or In Person
• Schools in Many Locations
• ESL by Distance Learning
• Multimedia Approach
   222-555-6584

Adult Community Center
▶ Free Classes
▶ Certified by State Education
▶ Conversational Approach
▶ Lowest Prices in Town
Dunmore......................555-2255

Better Language Workspace
Forget the Tapes! Forget the Videos! Learn from People!
Meet a Teacher Who Wants to Talk to You
Register online
www.betterlang.com
222-555-5588

CAPITAL AUDIO PROGRAMS
Learn a Language Conveniently:
Listen and Learn in your Home, Office, Car, Gym
A TEACHER IN A BOX
www.caplang.com • 222-555-9477

Computer Institute of America
Online Language Lessons
Full Program on CDs. All levels.
Learn at your convenience
and speed............222-555-0036

E C C Eastern Community College
Credit/Non-Credit Courses
Tuition assistance available
Classes Start:
Oct., Feb., May
11527 Golf Road,
Deer Lodge
555-5409

Executive
Language Center
BUSINESS ENGLISH PROGRAM
*Private lessons available
Visit for a
Free Trial Lesson*
222-555-9700

Phone Tronics
*The phone is your teacher
Private instruction on phone
Learn any time, any place*
1909 Kennedy Ave.,
Dunmore • 555-0234
L

Talk or Write

1. Which programs are free or partly free? How do you know?
2. Which listings seem good? Which schools would you need to call for more information? Which wouldn't you call? Why?
3. Choose the listing that seems most interesting to you. Does the ad give you enough information to make a choice? What questions would you ask if you called about that listing?
4. Have you or has someone you know ever chosen a business or service from the yellow pages? Was the experience bad or good? Explain.

Class Chat Walk around. Talk about when and where you have studied English. Ask what each classmate was doing then. Take notes. Complete a chart like the one below.

In 2002, I was studying English in a distance-learning program in San Diego. What were you doing then?

I was working in a store and studying to be a secretary in Guatemala.

I was studying English when/where?	Name	Was doing what/where?
In 2002 in San Diego	Alina	working and studying in Guatemala

Vocabulary

Circle new words. Brainstorm meanings and sample sentences. Take notes. List other words that you want to learn.

approach

compact disk (CD)

convenience

course

distance-learning

multimedia

convenient

online

private

Grammar Talk: Past Continuous

Willie felt nervous.
His wife and daughter **were planning** the wedding.
Willie felt nervous **when** his wife and daughter **were planning** the wedding.

I **was studying.**
My wife called some schools.
While I **was studying,** my wife called some schools.

We **were taking** the test from 9:00 to 10:00.
Sara arrived at 9:30.
When we **were taking** the test, Sara arrived.

Idiom Watch!

too good to be true

The simple past indicates an action that started and ended at a specific time in the past (last night, yesterday, in 2002).

The past continuous tells about an event that was happening at the same time as another event in the past.

Notice that the clauses in past continuous sentences can be in different orders. In which sentences above is the main clause first? In which sentence is the subordinate clause first?

When and while *are time words that are often used with the past continuous. What is the difference between these two words?*

Activity A Class Chat Follow-Up Use the information in your Class Chat chart to write sentences in your notebook about yourself and people in your class.

When I was studying English in San Diego in 2002, Alina was working and studying in Guatemala.

Activity B Look at the types of language schools in the listing on page 110. How many different language-learning approaches can you find? Make a list in your notebook. Then reread the list with a partner. If necessary, make changes to your list of language-learning approaches. Ask yourself the questions below, considering only language-learning approach. Don't consider cost or location.

• Which school would be your first choice? Why?
• Which school would be your last choice? Why?

Write your answers in a chart like this one. Talk about your answers with your group. Did everyone agree, or do different people prefer to learn in different ways? How could this information help you learn English better?

First-Choice School	Reason	Last-Choice School	Reason

 TASK 1: Make a Resource Guide

What do you want to know more about? Cooking? Plumbing? Computers? Money management? Brainstorm and do research with a partner or a small group of classmates who want to learn similar things. Follow these suggestions:

• Talk with other students, friends, teachers, and neighbors to find educational resources in your community.
• Look in the yellow pages for schools that might teach that subject.
• Look for flyers, community newspapers, and supermarket bulletin boards.
• Check nearby community colleges, YMCAs, and community centers.
• Research new technologies: studying online, with CDs, with audiotapes, or with videos. Check the Internet for ideas.
• Make an alphabetical list of all the resources that you find. Include phone numbers, addresses, web site addresses, and your comments.
• Share your guide with other students in your class.
• Your class may want to combine the resource lists from all the groups into a learning resource guide to share with other classes in the school.

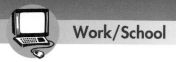

Working Out the Details

◆ Listen actively

◆ Think about lifelong learning in the US

What do *you* do when an English-speaking telephone salesperson tries to sell you something you don't want?

credit card
percent
shipping
video

◆ **Listening Tip** 🎧 When you talk to someone on the phone, focus your listening. Silence is a powerful learning tool. Don't rush to ask questions, disagree, or agree. Take your time and think about what you are hearing. Listen to this conversation between Willie and a salesperson. Focus your listening. The listening script is on page 139.

Willie had been thinking about a video language course. He's calling for information.

Talk or Write
1. What did you hear? What's the problem?
2. Do you think Willie's answers were good? Why or why not?
3. Check Willie's math. Is it correct? How much would the tapes cost at 20 percent off plus shipping?

What's Your Opinion? When is it OK to give your credit card number to someone over the phone or online? When is it not a good idea?

In the US Lifelong Learning and Self-Improvement

Most Americans believe that it's never too late to learn. Research shows that people who continue to learn, continue to grow mentally. Adults bring life experience with them when they go back to school. Adults know *what* they want to learn, and they often understand better than young people *how* they want to learn. Lifelong learning, sometimes called *continuing education,* is popular among people of all ages. There are many ways to learn—in a classroom, online, through a mentor, and with television or video courses.

Self-improvement programs are especially popular with Americans. Many people read books or join groups that help them manage time or money better, do better at their jobs, have better health, and so on.

☞ Compare Cultures

Lifelong learning is popular in the US, but not everywhere. In your group, talk about attitudes towards adult learning in other countries. Are there places in your home country where adults can take classes to improve their skills? If so, what are some popular things to study? What do you think about adult learning? Do you think that there is an age at which learning becomes difficult? If so, why do you think that happens? In your group, complete a chart like this one:

Positive Attitudes toward Lifelong Learning	Negative Attitudes toward Lifelong Learning

Vocabulary

Circle new words. Brainstorm meanings and sample sentences. Take notes. List other words that you want to learn.

misunderstand

outdo

preview

reconsider

continuing

fluent

insecure

lifelong

actively

mentally

Idiom Watch!

change your mind

Activity A With your class, find the meaning of the prefixes in the following words. Notice that prefixes can be added to nouns, verbs, or adjectives.

disrespect, **dis**miss   **micro**scope, **micro**wave   **out**do, **out**live   **re**live, **re**consider
inability, **in**secure   **mis**spell, **mis**understand   **pre**view, **pre**fix   **un**happy, **un**tie

Work with a partner to think of as many words as you can with these prefixes. Check your words in a dictionary or with an English speaker. By yourself, write a sentence using each word. Read your sentences to your partner. Then share your words and sentences with the class. Which pair of students has the most correct pairs of words and sentences?

One Step Up
Outside of class, listen and look for more words that have these prefixes. Report back to your group.

Activity B   Practice active listening. Read this list of questions with a partner. Each partner selects one question to talk about for two minutes.

- What is your personal experience with lifelong learning?

- Have you taken a continuing education class? What happened?

- Have you ever started to study something new and then stopped studying? What did you want to learn? Why didn't you continue?

- Do you believe that people grow mentally as they get older? Does mental growth depend on age or something else? What else?

- What has helped you grow mentally as an adult?

One Step Up

Outside of class, actively listen to a friend or family member talk, but don't tell the person what you are doing. First ask a question, and then really listen to the answer. Follow the rules for active listening. Report what happened to the class.

While one partner talks, the other listens actively. Follow these rules:

Rules for Active Listening

- Be silent for the whole two minutes.

- Look at the speaker.

- "Be there" mentally—thinking only about what the speaker is saying, *not* about other things.

- Ask the speaker at least one good question about what he or she said.

Talk about your experience with the class. How did it feel to really listen to someone? How did it feel to have someone give you his or her attention?

TASK 2:   Listening Actively to a Speaker

As a class, talk about people you know who are good models for lifelong learning—perhaps someone who learned a new skill or occupation later in life. Invite one or more of these people to be guest speakers in your class. Tell them when and for how long you want them to speak and what you want the speeches to be about. You can get some ideas from the questions in Activity B, or you can choose another aspect of lifelong learning.

When each person speaks, follow the rules for listening actively. At the end of the speech, ask questions. Record the speaker's answers in your notebook.

The next time you meet as a class, talk about each speech. What things did the speaker do well? What did you learn from the <u>content</u> (what the speaker said) and the <u>delivery</u> (how the speaker said it) of the speech?

✎💻 Technology Extra

Use a computer to publish a short summary of each speech. Add some of the best questions your class asked and the answers that the speaker gave. Title each summary "____ (speaker's name): A Lifelong-Learning Model." You may want to share your class summary with another class or post it on the school bulletin board.

Showing Your Pride

- ◆ Practice giving a short speech
- ◆ Use the past perfect continuous tense

Have you ever been worried about speaking in public?

◆ **Reading Tip** Speech writers often repeat similar words, phrases, or sentences to create a rhythm. Rhythm can make a speech more powerful and memorable. When you hear speeches, listen for these repetitions, or *parallel structures.* Willie has just written the first draft of his speech. As you read it, notice the parallel structures.

Words of Welcome

Welcome to you, my good friends and my dear family.

When Barbara and I came to this country, I thought I could not have been happier. But I was wrong.

When we had a beautiful daughter, an American daughter, I thought I could not have been happier. But I was wrong.

When Barbara and I became citizens, I thought I could not have been happier. But I was wrong.

When my daughter said she wanted to marry, I was happy. But when she asked me to give a speech at her wedding, I was also frightened. I wanted to say great things. But my English wasn't good. I had lots of problems communicating!

So I decided to go to Belmont Adult School to improve my English. They put me into the class of an excellent teacher. He knew that I had doubts about learning at my age. But he told me that we are never too old to learn. He showed me ways to learn that worked for me. I asked my teacher to write the speech for me. But he refused. He said I needed to express my own thoughts and feelings. I asked him to help me write a speech. But he refused. Instead he helped me find the English that I needed. Thanks to him, I found the way to say what is in my heart—and to say it in English.

This is the happiest day of my life. Life has been good to me. This country has been good to me. Now my daughter is getting married.

I wanted to say great things. But my English wasn't good.

Barbara and I look forward to a new stage in our relationship with her, and to our new relationship with . . .

Talk or Write

1. Give three reasons for Willie's happiness.
2. Have you ever made a speech on a special occasion? How did you feel?

Group Chat Willie had been wanting to improve his English. Tell your group about something that you had been wanting to do for a long time and finally did. Record your answers in a chart like the one below.

What did you do?

We had a baby. We had been wanting to have a baby for a long time.

What made you decide to do it?

We saved a lot of money last year.

Name	Event	Why?
Nelly	had a baby	saved a lot of money

Vocabulary

Circle new words. Brainstorm meanings and sample sentences. Take notes. List other words that you want to learn.

decide

guest

relationship

memorable

powerful

Grammar Talk: Past Perfect Continuous

You **had been worrying** about your speech.

We **had been trying** to pass the citizenship test.

The teacher **had been looking** for a chance to work with adult learners.

The past perfect continuous is used to talk about something that had been happening for some time in the past. What three verb forms are used in this tense?

Pronunciation Target • Disappearing Sounds and Syllables

🎧 *Listen to your teacher or the audio.*

The Missing r Sound

| February | governor | temperature | surprise |

When there are two rs in a long word, the first one often disappears.

The Missing v Sound in the Word of

| lots of problems | waste of time | box of rocks | bill of sale |

What sound do you hear for the word of?

The Disappearing Unstressed Vowel

| memorable | every | favorite | family |
| chocolate | interesting | restaurant | history |

How many syllables do you hear in each word?

Activity A Group Chat Follow-Up Use your Group Chat chart to write sentences. Write about the people in your group. Use the past perfect continuous.

Nelly and her husband had been wanting to have a baby.

Activity B With a partner, write sentences using the words with disappearing sounds on page 117. Use one or more of the words in each sentence.

In a restaurant, he always orders his favorite food, chocolate cake.

When you finish, read your sentences to your partner. Answer these questions:

1. Do syllables and sounds *always* disappear in these words?
2. Do Americans sometimes pronounce words like these more carefully?
3. Which pronunciation do you prefer? Why?

Activity C In speaking and in writing, it's good to use *synonyms,* different words that have the same meaning. Look back at Willie's speech. How many synonyms can you find for the word *good?* Write them in your notebook. Write a sentence with each synonym. With your class, write the synonyms on the board. Then each student writes a sentence under each synonym. Read the sentences together.

 TASK 3: Write a Speech

Write a speech honoring someone on a special occasion. Use the speech on the right as a model for yours. Follow these rules:

- Greet the guests and name the event.
- Congratulate the guest of honor and say a few special things about that person.
- Mention any other special guests.
- Add a little humor or advice.
- Thank the guests for coming and tell them to enjoy themselves.
- Know when to stop. People want to have fun, not listen to a long speech.

Memorize your speech or use a few notes written on one index card. It's important to look at the audience, not at your notes, when you speak. Practice saying your speech to a partner. Then present it to your group. Finally, keep your speech in a safe place. You may need it for a celebration soon!

> Welcome, friends, family, and most of all, my dear grandmother. I'm so happy to be here at the one hundredth birthday celebration for my grandmother. I know she's happy to be here. Maybe she's surprised to be here too. I'm not surprised because I know she is strong and wonderful.
>   At first she refused to come to her party. I know she did not want an elaborate celebration. She is modest. But she reconsidered, and here we all are at a simple party for her friends and family. As you can see, she has a lot of both. Happy birthday, dear grandmother.

◆ **Reading Tip**   When you read an article or a section of a book to get information, follow these four steps to active learning.

1. First **skim** the article, looking for the main points.

2. Then read the article again more slowly to **find examples and details** to support those points.

3. Next, **summarize** the article for yourself by writing the points that seem most important.

4. Finally, **evaluate** the points for yourself. Ask yourself these questions: Does it make sense? Was any information new to me? Did anything in the article change the way I think about the topic?

Now follow the steps as you read this article about the most common ways that adults learn.

ADULT LEARNING STYLES

Learning makes your brain stronger. When you learn something new, whether it's how to use a new word, how to snowboard, how to make a terrific chocolate dessert, or how to do a geometry problem, your brain is creating new connections. Your brain is also storing the information so you can find it when you need it.

This happens to you if you are 2, 22, or 82 years old. In fact, the more you learn, the stronger your brain gets. And the stronger your brain gets, the more you can learn.

People start learning the moment they are born. They continue to learn throughout their lives. Learning is truly a lifelong experience.

But how do we learn? Many educators believe that we each learn best in one of three different ways, or learning styles: **visual** (by seeing); **auditory** (by hearing and talking); or **tactile/kinesthetic** (by touching, moving, and doing). Tactile and kinesthetic learning styles used to be thought of as separate, but educators now think that they are so similar that they can be considered to be one learning style.

We all use all these styles at different times, but most of us have one *dominant*, or main, learning style. You may already have some idea of your dominant learning style.

If your dominant style is **visual:**

- You like to see a person speaking while you listen.

- You like to draw pictures to help you remember.

- You may prefer to learn by watching videos or films.

If your dominant style is **auditory:**

- You like to read, but you may understand and remember better if you read aloud.

- You prefer to learn by listening to what other people say.

- You easily remember things that people say to you.

- You often have mental conversations with yourself.

- You repeat words or sentences to yourself while listening.

Here's an interesting question: Do you think that reading is visual? Not all educators agree with this idea. Some say that although we see the words, we actually get the information by hearing ourselves say the words in our heads. For that reason many educators say that people who prefer to learn by reading are **auditory** learners.

If your dominant style is **tactile/ kinesthetic:**

- You need to move while you are learning.
- You like to work with tools.
- You are often distracted when you have to sit still to read or listen to discussions.
- You like to be active and explore the world around you.
- You want to touch things to understand what they are and how they work.

Sometimes it's possible to tell what kind of learner someone is by the way that person talks. A visual learner may say, "I see." An auditory learner may say, "I **hear** what you are saying." And a kinesthetic or tactile learner may say, "I **feel** that you are doing the right thing."

Not all of us had success learning as children and teenagers. Researchers now understand that this is often because we were being taught and made to learn in a way that didn't match our dominant learning style. Now, as an adult, if you can identify your learning style, you can find ways to learn better and enjoy learning.

A Learning Styles Quiz

Take this learning styles quiz by yourself. Answer each question by writing **T** for True or **F** for False. Work fast. Your first answer is usually the best and most honest one.

_____ 1. I like to listen to people talk.

_____ 2. I can easily remember what people say to me.

_____ 3. I like to learn by reading.

_____ 4. I sometimes talk to myself when I'm learning.

_____ 5. I often repeat what I hear or read to remember it better.

_____ 6. I sometimes draw pictures to help me remember things.

_____ 7. I enjoy learning by looking at maps and drawings.

_____ 8. The things I remember best are those I see.

_____ 9. I forget things that I am told to do.

_____ 10. I find it easy to remember what I see.

_____ 11. I can't sit in one place for long.

_____ 12. I enjoy drawing.

_____ 13. I like to work with tools.

_____ 14. I have to get up and move around when I study.

_____ 15. I need to take a lot of breaks when I study.

You will learn how to interpret your answers to this quiz on the next page.

Talk or Write

1. What are the three main learning styles described in this article?
2. How can these ideas about learning styles help explain why some people don't learn well in school?

Writing Task Create a "personal profile" of yourself. Write a paragraph about how you learn best. In your paragraph, you can include some of your answers from the quiz. You can also answer questions like these: Where do you study best? At what time of day? Do you like to study alone or with others? Do you enjoy music or quiet when you study? What special techniques do you think help you to learn?

Find Your Personal Learning Style

Knowing your personal learning style can help you learn. It can also help your teacher work with you. Now you will analyze your learning style and talk with other students who have the same style. You will consider ways to make your learning style work for you.

Get Ready

Complete the learning styles quiz on page 120. Count the number of *True* answers you had in each of the following sections:

Questions 1–5 _____

Questions 6–10 _____

Questions 11–15 _____

If you had the most *True* answers in . . .
- questions 1–5, you probably are an **auditory** learner.
- questions 6–10, you probably are a **visual** learner.
- questions 12–15, you probably are a **tactile/kinesthetic** learner.

If you had the same number of *True* answers in more than one group, you may be comfortable in more than one learning style. However, you still may prefer one style to the others. This is your dominant learning style.

Do the Work

Make these signs and post them in three parts of the room: *Visual, Auditory, Tactile/Kinesthetic.* Go to your dominant learning style area and do the following activities with other students who prefer the same style:

1. **Talk.** Discuss how you felt about the learning styles quiz. Were you surprised at the results? Do you agree with them? Were they the same as the personal profile you had written? Why or why not?
2. **Brainstorm.** With your group, list ways that people with your learning style can improve the way they study and learn.
3. **Write.** As a group, write a short list of suggestions or tips for students who have your learning style.

Present

1. In your group, organize a presentation to share your information and tips with the class.
2. As a class, make a poster with the learning styles quiz, a scoring chart, and the tips each group created.

Celebrating Success

Getting the Job You Want

Work/School
1

Home
2

Community
3

◆ **Vocabulary** Words for resumes • Words for job interviews

◆ **Language** Passive voice in simple present (review) • Verb tenses (review)

◆ **Pronunciation** Diphthongs • Syllable stress

◆ **Culture** Personal qualities admired in the US

When have you gotten work by telling people about things you can do well?

Martha has been on welfare for five years. She is frustrated. Although she has her GED, she can't find a job that pays enough to support herself and her son. Then an employment counselor at school tells her about a cleaning job with good pay. She wants the job, but she's worried. What will her family and friends say?

Think and Talk

1. What do you see in the picture?
2. Who is Martha talking to? What do you think they're talking about?
3. Do you know someone who accepted a job for which he or she felt overqualified? Why did the person take the job? What happened?
4. Do you know any people who said no to a job because they were worried about what other people would say? What happened?

What's Your Opinion? Should Martha take this cleaning job, even though she passed the GED test? Explain.

corporate

elite

maintenance

Gather Your Thoughts   With a partner, brainstorm ideas about how to use your personal qualities and experience to succeed. Ask yourself:

1. What are my best personal characteristics? How have I used them?
2. What employment skills have I learned at home? At school? At my previous jobs? As a volunteer? In another country?

Make an idea map like this one:

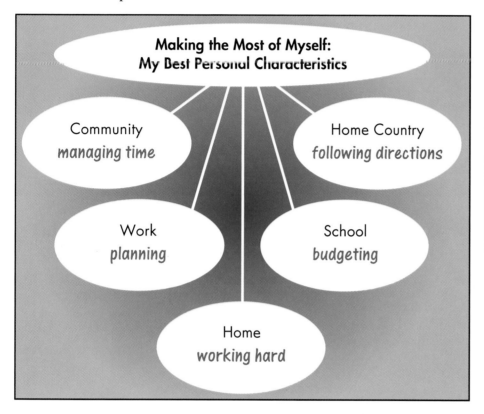

Now, in your group, try to agree on some characteristics of successful people.

What's the Problem? What could stop you from becoming successful? Think of three possible barriers to success. Write them in your notebook.

Setting Goals   Read the list of goals below. Then write another goal that is important to you. Rank the goals in order from 1 (most important) to 5.

_____ **a.** improve my employment skills

_____ **b.** spend more time with family or having fun

_____ **c.** continue my education

_____ **d.** do service in my community or religious group

_____ **e.** another goal: _____

Vocabulary

Circle new words. Brainstorm meanings and sample sentences. Take notes. List other words that you want to learn.

advancement

characteristic

effort

employment

image

obstacle

possibility

develop

overcome

overqualified

Idiom Watch!

make the most of yourself

One Step Up

As a class, use your group lists to talk about successful people. Then make a three-column class list or poster with the title: Successful People: Characteristics, Skills, Experiences.

Making the Most of Yourself

◆ Start a resume

◆ Use the passive voice in simple present

Would you like this job? Why or why not?

◆ **Reading Tip** Take time to think about your opinions as you read. As you read this flyer, ask yourself why Elite does or doesn't seem like a good place to work.

Are You Ambitious? Do You Want a Secure Future?

Who Are We? We are the best and most reliable cleaning service in town. We clean offices at some of the most successful companies in our community. ELITE was started by a single parent who wanted to spend time with her children. She wanted a flexible schedule. She also needed to make a living. She started her own small cleaning business. She cleaned carefully. She hired others who took the same pride in their work. It grew into a large business. Now a flexible schedule and great benefits are available to you if you can meet our high standards.

Come visit us at ELITE. Call us at 555-2376 to learn more.

Don't stay at your low-paying job another minute.

Join ELITE CORPORATE MAINTENANCE SERVICE today.

Job Description: Office Cleaner
Duties:

• Nightly: Dust desks, vacuum all rugs and carpets. Dry-mop floors. Empty wastebaskets.

• Weekly: Wet-mop floors. Clean glass windows and mirrors. Vacuum upholstery. Dust lightbulbs and lamps.

Requirements: You must …

• be honest (We do a background check on each employee.)

• have three references: two personal, one professional

• have cleaning experience

• be hard-working and ambitious

We offer a flexible schedule, great benefits, and plenty of room for advancement. Fax or e-mail your resume to Elite Corporate Maintenance Service. No phone calls or snail mail, please.

Talk or Write

1. What should someone do to apply for this job?
2. What are the duties of the office cleaner?
3. Give three reasons why Elite might be a good company to work for.
4. What is the difference between personal and professional references? Why does the flyer ask for both?

What's Your Opinion? Why do cleaning services do a background check on people who work for them? Would you agree to a background check?

Remember?

benefits

Group Chat List every job, paid or unpaid, that each group member has had. Take turns asking and answering the questions in a chart like the one below. List all the information in the chart. Report to the class.

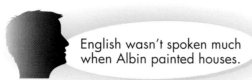

English wasn't spoken much when Albin painted houses.

What's your name?	What jobs have you had?	What were your duties?	Was English spoken?
Albin	painter, cook, newspaper salesman, candy maker	As a painter, I painted houses, repaired walls, and cleaned up.	Not much.

Vocabulary

Circle new words. Brainstorm meanings and sample sentences. Take notes. List other words that you want to learn.

background

duty

reference

ambitious

flexible

honest

reliable

secure

Grammar Talk: Passive Voice in Simple Present

<u>Active</u>	<u>Passive</u>
Mega Corporation **employs** many people.	Many people **are employed** by Mega Corporation.
The mail carrier **delivers** the packages.	The packages **are delivered** by the mail carrier.
People in the Bahamas **speak** English.	English **is spoken** by people in the Bahamas.

The subject in an active sentence becomes the object of a preposition in a passive sentence. Is the by *phrase always needed in a passive sentence?*

The passive voice in simple present is formed with a present tense form of the verb be (am, is, *or* are) + *past participle.*

Idiom Watch!

make a living

single parent

Pronunciation Target • Diphthongs

🎧 *Listen to your teacher or the audio.*

b<u>uy</u> [ay]   empl<u>oy</u> [oy]   backgr<u>ou</u>nd [ow]

A vowel sometimes combines with a vowel sound near it to make a new sound. In this **diphthong,** *two vowel sounds combine. Now pronounce each of the following words after your teacher several times. Feel how your mouth moves when you say the sound. Can you describe how it moves?*

pie, lie, guy   toy, enjoy, choice   house, blouse, bough

Activity A **Group Chat Follow-Up** Analyze the information from your Group Chat. With your class, think of ways to categorize the jobs that you and your classmates have had. Make a class chart like the one below. Put the initials of each classmate after the job that person had. If necessary, change or add headings to make the chart fit the kinds of jobs you and your classmates have had.

Health Services	Office Work	Food Services	Other:

When you have finished your chart, talk about these questions:
- What kinds of jobs did most class members have?
- Who do you think had the most unusual job?
- Who has had the most jobs?
- What did this categorizing activity tell you about your classmates or about jobs in the area where you live?

Activity B Change these sentences from active to passive. Write the new sentences in your notebook. If you think the *by* phrase is not necessary in a sentence, leave it out.

1. Elite cleans offices and homes.   *Offices and homes are cleaned by Elite.*

2. Someone vacuums the rugs.   *Rugs are vacuumed.*

3. Someone mops the floors.

4. Another person dusts the desks and tables.

5. Two people wash the windows.

6. The supervisor checks all cleaning jobs.

7. They clean your house until it shines.

As a class, talk about which sentences need the *by* phrase and which don't.

 TASK 1: Prepare to Write a Resume

Write about all jobs listed for you in the Group Chat. This can be paid or unpaid work, including housework, study, volunteering, working for relatives, caring for children, or looking for a job. In your notebook, write this information about each job:
- job title
- company and/or location
- job description and duties
- supervisor
- length of time on job
- skills used on job
- what you liked
- what you didn't like

Making Your Work History Count

◆ Prepare a work history

◆ Learn about personal qualities that are valued in the US

What skills have you developed from family activities? Should you include those skills on your resume?

◆ **Reading Tip**   When you read information with many details, each detail may not tell you much, but you can put those details togcthcr to form a more complete picture. Read these notes that Martha wrote about her experience. Does this list of accomplishments tell you what kind of person Martha is?

Job 1: 4th of July Food Committee Chairperson
Ordered food
Made budget
Trained volunteers
Assigned them jobs
Organized clean-up
Applied for permit from park

Job 3: Parents' Association Treasurer
250 members-collected dues, kept records
Reported on budget to members
Authorized expenses
(Learned a little about computers!)

Job 2: Home health aide (part-time for agency)
Did light cleaning and housekeeping
Shopped, cooked
Organized drawers and closets
Read to older woman; took her for walks
(Good job, but I had to quit when my son was born.)

I know I can do the job, but I need to make my experience count.

Talk or Write

1. Which of Martha's jobs were paid and unpaid? Explain your answers.
2. What can you tell about Martha from reading her notes? What positive personal qualities does she seem to have?
3. Have you ever used home or volunteer experience to qualify for a paid job? If so, what was the experience? How did it help you? If not, can you think of unpaid experience that you could have used?

What's Your Opinion? Do you think it's OK to include unpaid work experience on your resume? Should you explain that it was unpaid?

Pronunciation Target • Syllable Stress

🎧 *The word* permit *can be a noun or a verb depending on which syllable is stressed.* PerMIT *is a verb.* PERmit *is a noun. Listen to your teacher pronounce the two words. Repeat them. As a class, list other pairs of words whose stress changes in the same way.*

Vocabulary

Circle new words. Brainstorm meanings and sample sentences. Take notes. List other words that you want to learn.

permit

assertive

eager to learn

hard-working

high-achieving

honest

optimistic

organized

persevering

self-reliant

In the US   Personal Qualities That Americans Like

Americans like and admire certain qualities in people. American employers like to see those qualities in people who work for them. Look again at the words in the vocabulary box. The adjectives are all qualities that Americans admire. If your work history and resume show that you have these qualities, this can help you look good to companies. As a class, talk about the meanings of any words you don't know. Think or talk about how you can present your experience in a resume to show that you have many of these personal qualities.

Idiom Watch!
make something count

☛ Compare Cultures

Tell group members what success means for people in one country that you know about. Are the ways in which success is measured similar to or different from ways in the US? Do you agree with the measures of success in that country? Why or why not? What do you think are some good measures of success?

Activity A   On page 127, you listed some of Martha's personal qualities. Now think again, as you began to do on page 123, about your own good personal qualities. Are you ambitious? Hard-working? A good friend? A good teacher? What else?

Each person sits in the center of the class for one minute. The rest of the class tells that person about his or her personal qualities. Say good and true things about each of your classmates for one minute. Try to use some of the words in the vocabulary box. When it's your turn, enjoy hearing good things about yourself. Take notes about your personal qualities on a star-shaped idea map like the one on the right.

Discuss with your group: How did it feel to hear only good things about yourself for a minute? Were you surprised by any of the personal qualities that your classmates said you had?

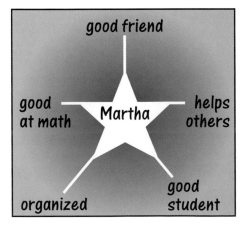

One Step Up
Make a list of your best personal qualities in your notebook.

Activity B With a partner, look at the job description on page 124. List all the personal qualities needed for the cleaning job on the left side of a two-column chart. Then look at the list of Martha's personal qualities from question 2 on page 127. Write her personal qualities on the right side. Report back to your group. Start by saying, "I think she's qualified for this job because she's _____."

Activity C Practice an interview. Look at the star-shaped idea map that you made of your own personal qualities. Talk to your partner about yourself. Start by saying, "(Someday) I want a job as a _____. I think I'm qualified for the job because I'm _____." Don't be shy. In an interview, people need to act proud of their personal qualities and their experience.

Activity D Review the present passive. Tell your group about a meeting or event that you attend regularly. It could be a religious service, a parent association meeting, a town or neighborhood meeting, a weight-loss group, and so on. Use the present passive to tell about it. Are speeches made? Are refreshments served? Is the meeting attended by many people? Where is it usually held? After each person speaks, the group works together to write a short paragraph about the meeting.

TASK 2: Start a Work History

In your notebook, provide the information listed below about *all* the jobs you or someone you know has had.

1. Job
2. Location/address
3. When job began
4. How long you had job
5. Duties
6. Most difficult part of job
7. Positive and negative features of job
8. Name and title of immediate supervisor
9. When you left job and reason for leaving
10. What you learned from job
11. Possible contact at or reference from that workplace

Remember?

Active: They serve refreshments.
Passive: Refreshments are served.
Active: Many people attend the meetings.
Passive: The meetings are attended by many people.

One Step Up

Use some of the questions to interview someone who is working at a job that interests you or who has had an interesting job in the past. Take notes. Use them to write a paragraph about the job or jobs.

✎💻 Technology Extra

Do Internet research. Look up the web site of a large company that you know or have heard about. It could be one of the companies that you or someone you know worked for in the past. Take notes about the most interesting fact you find on the web site. Report what you learned to the class.

Making a Good Impression

◆ Prepare for a job interview

◆ Review verb tenses

---

administrative

belongings

clerical

conflict resolution

unfamiliar

valuable

Could you answer questions in an interview today? If not, what steps would you need to take first?

◆ **Listening Tip** 🎧 If you don't understand an interview question, it's fine to ask the interviewer to repeat or speak more slowly. Another way to understand interview questions better is to focus your listening. As you listen to Martha's interview, do some focused listening by concentrating on the questions that the interviewer asks. List at least some of those questions as you listen. The listening script is on page 140.

Martha is interviewing for a cleaning job.

MARTHA BERNARD

125 E. Amsterdam Ave.
Brooklyn, NY 11733
(718) 555-8713

Talk or Write

1. What kind of information does Martha have to provide?
2. Which questions were easy to understand? Which questions would you find most difficult to answer?
3. Would you change any answer made by Martha? How?
4. How would you prepare for this kind of interview? Explain.

Group Chat   In a group, describe the work that you've done in the past. Use action words like these: *coordinated . . . managed . . . initiated . . . supervised . . . produced . . . built . . . solved . . . recruited . . . provided . . . ,* etc. Be sure to include examples that describe work you did at home or in your neighborhood. Have a group recorder organize the answers on a chart like the one below.

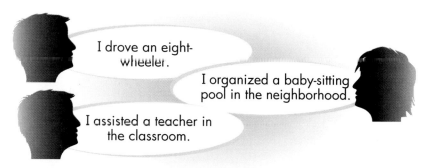

I drove an eight-wheeler.

I organized a baby-sitting pool in the neighborhood.

I assisted a teacher in the classroom.

Name	What did the person do?
Tom	drove an eight-wheeler

Vocabulary

Circle new words. Brainstorm meanings and sample sentences. Take notes. List other words that you want to learn.

> concern
>
> criticism
>
> appreciate
>
> specify
>
> train
>
> competent
>
> impressed
>
> limited
>
> trustworthy

Activity A   Group Chat Follow-Up Practice with the jobs and action words from the Group Chat. In your group, change the verb in each sentence to make new sentences. Use as many verb tenses from the chart on page 132 as you can, adding words to give the sentences more meaning. For example, you could change the sentence "Tom drove an eight-wheeler" as follows:

- Tom **has driven** an eight-wheeler for five years. (present perfect)
- Tom **had driven** an eight-wheeler on his last job. (past perfect)

One Step Up

For more practice, exchange your Group Chat chart with other groups in your class.

 TASK 3:   Prepare for a Job Interview

Tell your group about three personal goals you have achieved. These can be goals related to employment, your personal life, or involvement in the community. Tell what actions you took to achieve each goal. Describe each accomplishment on a 3 × 5 card. Include the following:

Challenge: What you needed to do. Why you needed to do it. The issues and problems you had to deal with.

Actions: What you did. (Use active verbs like *planned, saved, changed, moved, developed,* etc.)

Results: What you achieved. Whenever possible, use words that measure things. Tell how much money was saved or what percent improved. Try to describe the results with specific experiences.

Grammar Talk: Verb Tense Review

This chart reviews seven verb tenses that are often used.

	Affirmative Statement	Negative Statement	Question
Simple Present	I **am** concerned about it.	He **is not** trustworthy.	**Are** they competent?
	Martha **wants** a job.	Ana **doesn't like** criticism.	**Do** you **react** well to criticism?
Present Progressive	I**'m being** optimistic.	Ray **is not being** helpful.	**Are** you **being** assertive?
	We**'re looking** for a job.	Joe **is not talking** about his job.	**Are** they **preparing** a budget?
Be + Going to + verb	He**'s going to be** treasurer.	The effort **is not going to be** worth it.	**Are** there **going to be** obstacles?
	They**'re going to vote** for a chairperson.	He**'s not going to succeed.**	**Are** you **going to face** them?
Simple Past	Possibilities **were** good.	Lila **wasn't** overqualified.	**Was** your mother a single parent?
	He **developed** his best characteristics.	They **didn't offer** many benefits.	**Did** she **list** her references?
Future	I **will be** responsible for the duties.	She **will not be** an assertive candidate.	**Will** these children **be** optimistic and self-reliant?
	Now Tuan **will earn** a good living.	Their situation **will not help** them get more aid.	**Will** you **receive** the message by snail mail?
Present Perfect	As workers, they **have been** eager to learn.	I **haven't been** lonely here without you.	**Have** you **been** to this agency before?
	This year, I**'ve trained** six people in this company.	Carol **hasn't used** her car for weeks now.	**Have** you **stated** which kind of work you want?
Past Perfect	Amy **had been** sick.	Martha **hadn't been** optimistic about the job.	**Had** the personnel department **been** fair?
	I **had traveled** in South America during those years.	My parents **hadn't arrived** in the US in 1975.	**Had** the brothers **attained** high-level jobs?

What verb is in the first sentence in every pair? The second sentence in each pair has a regular verb. Notice that some sentences include long forms, while others include contractions. Take a few minutes to look at the chart again. Which tenses do you think you need most to review?

◆ **Reading Tip**   Knowing the source of your reading may prepare you better for information introduced in the reading. The article below came from an advice column. Is the writer accurate and believable? Why? What do you think of Annabelle's writing style? What have you read that was written in a similar style?

Workplace Section

Ask Annabelle
Looking for a job? Can't find one?

 Annabelle solves your most difficult career problems.

Dear Annabelle:

I have sent out over 100 resumes. I haven't gotten even one answer. What's going on?

How are interviewees chosen? How do they select people to interview? My friend told me that they throw the resumes into the air and read the first 10 that reach the floor. Is that true?

Jobless in Johnstown

Dear Jobless:

Yes, I have heard the one about throwing resumes in the air. It's just not true. If it were true, one of your 100 resumes might have gotten you a phone call by now. Your question is a good one. Just how are people chosen for jobs? I talked with personnel managers at 10 big companies about what makes a resume a "loser." Here are the things they do *not* want to see in a resume.

- **Messy.** Would you believe it? Coffee stains, whiteout, crossed-out words. Just plain ugly. Your resume is your introduction. You wouldn't wear a wrinkled shirt to an interview. Don't send a wrinkled resume.

---

accurate

conservative

down = sad

fasten your seatbelt = be prepared for an exciting experience

figure out = make sense of

fonts = styles of type

the one = the story, the joke

...*Ask Annabelle*

- **Too long.** You may find the details of your life exciting, but a busy personnel manager wants the facts in a clear, simple form.
- **Too complicated.** Have a friend read your resume for you. If that person can't figure out what you've been doing for the past five years, you need to do some rewriting.
- **Not targeted for the job.** If the job description is for a lifeguard, don't emphasize your amazing computer experience. It's nice to tell companies that you have other skills and abilities, but stay focused on the job you're applying for.
- **Poor spelling and grammar.** They have to be perfect. If yours aren't, get a friend or teacher to check your draft.
- **Busy, busy, busy.** Yes, we are happy that you have lots of fonts on your computer, but this is not the time to use them all. No color, no pictures. White or beige paper. It's best to be conservative.

Annabelle

Dear Annabelle:

I had a friend read my resume and she said it was OK, but "flat." What does that mean? How can I fix a flat resume?

Down in Denver

Dear Down:

Your friend wasn't talking about the air in your tires. She was telling you, in a nice way, that your resume is boring, boring, boring. Don't worry. You can fix it with some strong, lively verbs. For example, which one of these phrases "sells" the writer and convinces the reader better— "Did filing" or "Developed an efficient filing system that saved the company time and money"?

Here are some strong verbs that you can use in your resume: *developed, created, planned, prepared, budgeted, advised, implemented.* Look them up in a dictionary if you don't know their meanings. Practice using them. Add one or two to your resume. When your friend reads it again, tell her to fasten her seatbelt.

Annabelle

P.S. Notice that the verbs are all in the past tense. If you're writing about your present job, use the present tense, but remember that all your past work experience is past, OK?

That's it for now. Don't forget to write to me if you need advice on job hunting. I'm here for you.

Annabelle Marti

Talk or Write

1. What do you think was the best advice Annabelle gave?
2. Do you think Annabelle's ideas are right? Give your reasons.
3. Were these letters easy to read? Why or why not?

Writing Task Write one of your own resume-related questions for a job-advice column. Then, as a class, put all the questions in a box. Each student chooses one to answer in the way that an advice columnist would. Write a serious answer using what you know, including the things you learned in this unit. Each student will read the question and his or her answer to the class. As a class, discuss the advice.

Prepare a Resume

To be ready for job opportunities, prepare an up-to-date resume.

Get Ready

1. Get a Resume Preparation Form from your teacher.
2. Review the work you did for Task 1 and Task 2.
3. Collect any additional information you will need to complete the form.

Do the Work

1. Fill out the top of the form with your personal information.
2. Write your qualifications on the lines provided. Remember to start with descriptive words such as "well-organized," "bilingual in _____ and English," "honest and reliable."
3. Start with your current job experience. Go back to Task 1 to review.
4. Describe your past work experience on the next two or three sections. Remember to use action words to list your skills and responsibilities.
5. Enter information about your education.
6. Type up your resume.
7. Use this checklist to revise and improve your resume. Have you
   - included all the information needed to identify yourself?
   - listed your employment experience with the most recent job first?
   - given the dates each job began and ended, your job title, and the name of the company?
   - described your responsibilities?
   - listed work-related experience that demonstrates your skills?
   - described your education?
   - written "References available on request"?
   - obtained permission from at least three people who will provide references for you?

Present

1. Before using your resume in an interview, show it to your teacher or someone else in your support network. Ask for comments and suggestions. Make changes.
2. Practice your presentation many times until you can do it perfectly. You don't have to memorize your resume, but use the information to support your interview answers.
3. Put your resume into a portfolio along with copies of diplomas, special licenses, or certificates.

Listening Scripts

UNIT 1
Taking the First Step

Lesson 1, page 12

Grandmother: Your grandfather gave me this music box. I've listened to it play for the last 50 years. No matter where I've been, when I've heard this music, I've felt both happy and sad.

Patria: So are you glad that you came to the US?

Grandmother: I've had a wonderful life here, and the best part of it is knowing that your life will be even better than mine.

Patria: How do you know that? My friend Jack has always told me that making a better life takes planning and hard work, not just dreaming.

Grandmother: I've just always known it. Here, look at this. What is it?

Patria: It looks like a diploma. You never told me that you graduated from a special school.

Grandmother: It's for a course on natural medicines that I took a long time ago. I wanted to continue studying, but I couldn't. Still, I've taught myself much more about plants and herbs since then—how to use them to help people feel healthy.

Patria: So what else did you want to study?

Grandmother: I dreamed of being a nurse. I went to school for just a little while, met and married your grandfather, became a mother, and found a new dream in the US. I took a chance coming here, and I'm glad that I did. I'm not a nurse, but I've helped lots of people. And I've had many dreams come true. And what about you, Patria?

Patria: You've taught me everything you know about plants. You predicted that I would help people with my knowledge and maybe even become famous. That gave me a dream of my own.

Grandmother: Thank you, Patria. I . . . I guess I never realized that I'd helped you.

Patria: You really did. When I was in high school, I always dreamed of being a botanist. But, you know, I have to admit that working in the cafeteria at the Botanical Garden has been a dead-end job for me. The people are nice, the work isn't hard, but I haven't been learning or growing. And for that reason, my dream began to seem so . . . so difficult. Sometimes I didn't even know how to begin. But I knew that I had to make it happen myself.

Grandmother: I know your dream will come true. I predict it.

Patria: Listen, sometimes your predictions come true and sometimes they don't, right? That's why I can't just dream. Some people can plan, but they never dream. Some people can dream, but they never plan. It's been good for me to dream, to see my long-term goals, but now I have to spend time planning carefully to make that dream come true. I've begun to think about all the steps I need to take. I've talked with other people and I've read some books. But to be successful, I need to keep on planning and working hard—working for years—until I finally reach my goal of being a botanist.

Grandmother: You'll find a way. But I don't want you to work as hard as I did. I want your life to be wonderful.

Patria: Working hard can be wonderful if you really love what you're working at. You'll see— sooner than you think.

UNIT 2
Selling Your Skills

Lesson 1, page 26

Narrator: Hassam and his wife, Masa, have invited a friend to their apartment to ask for advice. Hassam has an interview at an art gallery, and he wants to present himself and his work in the best way possible. Hassam's friend has a lot of experience interviewing.

Hassam: Peter, let's talk. You know, if my meeting with Ms. Patterson goes well tomorrow, she'll try to sell some of my work.

Peter: Do you have something to show her?

Hassam: If I had more time, I could make these photos of my work look more professional.

Peter: We never have enough time, Hassam. If you use what you have here, you'll do just fine.

Hassam: You're probably right. So do you think that if I added a little color to the photos, they would look better?

Peter: That's a good idea. Also, if I were you, I'd label each photo. You can make some nice labels and titles on your computer. By the way, these little cakes are delicious, Masa. You're so busy working in the bakery, how can you find time to bake at home?

Masa: They're good, but if I had the right ingredients, they would taste more like they do in Egypt. You know, you're right, Peter. I don't have much time for anything except my work. If Hassam sold some of his paintings, maybe we could take a vacation to see our families. We've both worked very hard these last two years.

Hassam: That's for sure. But let's get back to *my* problem. I really want to make a good impression tomorrow. I've prepared a resume. Any more suggestions, Peter?

Peter: Have you thought about what you're going to say to Ms. Patterson? You know, the way you present yourself is as important as your skills.

Hassam: I'm wondering what I should wear. Would I look too formal if I wore my new blue suit?

Peter: Good question. Let's talk about that.

UNIT 3
Getting Help

Lesson 1, page 40

Anna: Raising a teenager these days is very difficult.

Bob: I know. I sometimes feel like I'm losing control of my daughter. Everything I say is always wrong. Sometimes I just want to give up and let her do anything she wants. Then she'll learn her lesson!

Bonnie: I know how you feel, but we can't give up on them. They have to know we're there, paying attention to them.

Anna: Well, Erin stopped listening to me a long time ago. Since she met this boy, she's not the same person that she was. We used to talk about everything, but now she seems to be hiding something from me. And she's not paying attention to her schoolwork, so I'm worried.

Bonnie: Do you know this boy? Who is he?

Anna: I've met him a few times. He seems nice enough. He smiles and acts polite when he's in my home.

Bob: It's too bad we can't see how they act when they're *not* with us.

Anna: I don't trust that boy— maybe because he's *too* nice. Maybe he's trying to hide something. Once I thought that I smelled alcohol on his breath.

Bonnie: Well, what does Erin say?

Anna: Not much. When I asked her if he was drinking, she got very upset and started to yell at me.

Bob: Oh boy! She may be in a situation where you need to step in. If I were you I would stop her from going out with him.

Bonnie: That won't work. At her age, you can't just stop her. Be careful, she might keep seeing him just because you told her not to.

Anna: You know, I'm really scared for her. I suspect that sometimes he's violent. I think Erin is scared too, but I'm afraid to ask her.

Bonnie: Why do you say that he might be violent?

Anna: Well, I noticed some bruises on her arm yesterday. But she didn't want to talk about it.

Bonnie: You really should try to find help, Anna. You probably need to go to the police to get protection for your daughter.

Bob: That doesn't always help. You really should get out of the neighborhood. Get out, as far as possible. This is no joke. It's serious business.

Anna: Oh! I don't know what to do. I really have to have a talk with Erin. I can't ignore this problem any longer.

UNIT 4
On Your Own

Lesson 1, page 54

Announcer: We've just been talking with Kimberly Corby Cooper, retired businesswoman and volunteer mentor for small businessmen and -women who are just getting started. She told us a story about her career that was really inspiring. Kim, tell us, what advice do you have right now for a listener who wants to start his or her own business?

Kim: Ralph, I would say, "Go for it!" A man or woman who enjoys being creative and independent will enjoy having a small business. And actually the small business is not just a good way to become independent but also a good way to help other people. Did you know that most new jobs created in the US are in small businesses? Did you know that small businesses in the United States employ 51 percent of the workforce? The US Department of Commerce reported 9,907,000 self-employed people in 2001. Besides that, . . .

Announcer: Wait a minute, Kim. This sounds too good. There must be some problems.

Kim: Oh, yes. In fact, according to the US Small Business Administration, over half of all new businesses fail within the first five years.

Announcer: So this wouldn't be good for a person who needs a lot of security. Right?

Kim: No indeed. When my first company, which provided temporary secretaries, failed, I felt terrible. But I learned a lot. My second small business, which does office cleaning throughout the city, was very successful.

Announcer: Do you have any advice for a person who wants to get started?

Kim: Yes, I do. Persistence pays, so don't give up. Learn from your mistakes and move on.

Announcer: That's about all the time we have . . .

Donna: I can't listen to this anymore. Didn't you hear her say that over 50 percent of all small businesses fail? That's *half,* Sheba!

Sheba: I heard that 50 percent of all businesses succeed. *That's* half. I guess it depends on how you look at it. I thought her message was inspiring. Look at me, Donna. I'm a woman who came from Ethiopia. I did OK. I'll help you . . . *if* you really want to take the big step.

Donna: I want to, really.

Sheba: OK then. Let's get started.

UNIT 5
Think before You Buy!

Lesson 1, page 68

Narrator: Bill is talking with his friends at school after class at the community college.

Bill: OK, guys, I need help. My old camera is broken and the warranty is expired. I spent a long time trying to figure out what to do with it, but I'm going to need to buy a new one, and, as usual, until I finish school and get a good job, I'm on a tight budget. Can you come up with ideas for how and where I could buy a new camera?

Keith: I've got an old camera. Want to buy it?

Bill: No, thanks! This time, I'd like to get a new, high-quality piece of equipment—but I want a good deal. Have any of you bought a camera lately? What do I need to know before I walk into a store?

Deborah: Well, you don't even need to walk into a store to make a purchase. You can find bargains on the Web. There are also special product magazines that have good information and ads for cameras that you order through an 800 number or, again, through a Web address. And, of course, there are the general consumer publications.

Bill: OK, but you know that I'm no expert on cameras. I don't want to read really technical explanations.

Keith: Well, one thing you need to think about is whether you want a traditional or a digital camera.

Bill: If I have a digital one, I can send pictures over the Web, right? And I won't need to buy film. But that's actually really all I know.

Steve: Best thing you can do then, Bill, is to go to the library and read the latest issues of the consumer magazines. They'll tell you about the features and the advantages and disadvantages of each type of camera. They keep the explanations simple because they know the average reader is not a technical genius.

Deborah: Yeah, and they'll also rate different brands. It's a really good and easy way to do research when you want to buy a new product.

Keith: Also, sometimes they tell you which products are the best bargains—or the best buy for the money.

Bill: So once I research the possibilities and choose the camera I want, where do you think I can get the best price?

Deborah: Sometimes online prices are better than prices in stores. But big discount stores can have really good prices too. You can check prices at comparison-shopping web sites. You might try doing a computer search for words like *shopper, shopping,* and then maybe the combination *camera* and *shopping.*

Bill: I see I've got some work to do. Thanks for all your help!

UNIT 6
Protecting Your Rights

Lesson 2, page 85

Welcome to the City Small Claims Court information line. To listen to this message in English, press 1. For Spanish, press 2. To listen to this message in other languages, press 3. If you do not have a Touch-Tone phone or if you need to talk to an operator, press zero or stay on the line, and someone will help you.

Listen to the following information before filing a claim. Press the pound key to have the message repeated.

Before filing a claim, you must contact the other person to discuss and try to resolve the problem. You must make sure the person knows you are going to sue.

Filing a claim: You can file a claim in this court if the amount in dispute is $5,000 or less. The filing fee is $20. You can get claims forms at the Municipal Building.

Small Claims Court works quickly and will schedule your case within 40 days.

Typical cases filed in Small Claims Court are auto accidents, property damage, landlord/tenant disputes, and collecting money owed.

A Small Claims Court judge will hear your case. Bring to court any papers, photos, contracts, or other things that support your case. You may also bring witnesses. You—the plaintiff, or the person suing—speak first. The defendant, or the person you are suing, can also present evidence. It's up to you to prove your case.

The judge may decide the case immediately or may mail the decision to you later.

Press the pound key to hear this message again.

UNIT 7
Participating in Your Community

Lesson 3, page 102

Mr. Schuler: Ladies and gentlemen, as you know, we are completing plans to build a new low-income housing project in the area between Clark and Elwood Streets. We have contracted our local builders already, and the work will begin this summer. I know that many of you are concerned about this project. I will try to answer your questions this evening. I know that members of our opposition have made you worry and fear what may happen. But I promise you that this project will solve many of the problems this community has faced for years. It will *not*, I repeat, *not,* create more problems. (brief pause) I will take your questions now.

Audience Member 1: Mr. Schuler, how do you plan to solve the problem of our high school, which is already overcrowded? Won't the student population increase when the families move into the housing project?

Mr. Schuler: Those families are already here in our neighborhood, and their children already attend our schools. The conditions they live in are terrible. The new houses will improve these conditions. But the student population will not increase much more than what we already expected, based on higher elementary school and middle school enrollments. To make room for more students, we have already begun to move the school district headquarters out of the high school and into a new location. This will create more classroom space for all our children.

Audience Member 2: I am very concerned about the value of my home. I'm worried that it will go down because of the project. I've seen many FOR SALE signs near the high school. People are already running away.

Mr. Schuler: Unfortunately, our opposition has said many exaggerated and untrue things about this project. This has caused a small number of individuals to leave our community. But this town has a wonderful history of tolerance. It is a town that cares! We have grown successfully over the years, and we will continue to do so in the future!

Audience Member 3: How do you respond to the person who said that some town council members sold their own homes as soon as the proposal for this project was approved?

Mr. Schuler: One council member did sell her house. I'm sorry she couldn't be here tonight to answer your question, but she and I have talked about this ridiculous comment. The timing of her sale was merely a coincidence. She put her house up for sale as soon as her children had all started college, just at the time this project was approved.

Audience Member 4: Mr. Schuler, as parents we are very concerned about a possible rise in crime around the high school. We have seen that the overcrowded conditions in projects in neighboring towns have created an environment where drug activity and other types of crime have gotten out of control.

Mr. Schuler: When we planned our project, we paid special attention to the mistakes made by our neighbors. For one thing, we have taken steps to prevent overcrowding in this project. We have provided more plot space for each house. Every house will have a front and a back yard, and there will be good space between the houses. The project will look like a small village, not a typical city project.

Audience Member 5: What about the people who will live in these houses? I've seen lots of beautiful housing ruined in a year by the people who moved in.

Mr. Schuler: When we say low-income, we mean just that. These people *have* income. They are hard-working, just like you and me. They struggle, just as you and I do. They are young people, old people, people who normally wouldn't be able to afford a new house because of high costs at this time. They are good people, like you and me, who need a chance to make a good life for their families. (pause) Are there other questions? No? If not, I want to thank you for coming and for your interest in our community. (applause). Thank you very much, my friends.

UNIT 8
It's Never Too Late

Lesson 2, page 113

Salesman: Hello. You've reached Embassy Video Learning. Were you thinking about improving your English? Well, we have a program that can outdo any competitor's—only 12 tapes to fluent English. How can I help you?

Willie: I want to improve my English pronunciation and grammar.

Salesman: Let me tell you that you've called the right place at the right time. Give me your name, address, and credit card number. In three days you will receive the 12 tapes, and, believe me, you'll never feel insecure about your English again. You can preview the tapes for 30 days and . . .

Willie: Excuse me. I have some questions.

Salesman: Of course you do. Tape 1 of the video learning program will help you ask those questions in perfect English. Just give me your name, address, and credit card number and you will receive the first tape, "Asking and Answering Questions in the Present Tense."

Willie: How much is it?

Salesman: Just $3.95 plus shipping.

Willie: That's a good price for 12 tapes.

Salesman: $3.95 is for the first tape. The others are $19.95 each.

Willie: Hmmm. I misunderstood. Well—11 times $19.95 is . . . let me see . . . $219.45 plus $3.95 for the first one makes it $223.40. How much is the shipping?

Salesman: It depends on where you live. Usually about five dollars a tape.

Willie: So each tape is . . . just a minute, uh . . . $24.95.

Salesman: I can see you don't need Tape 6, "Learning English for Math Problems."

Willie: I have my own business, and I need to be good at numbers. I'd been thinking about studying at home with videos. But I changed my mind. It's too expensive. Thank you. Goodbye.

Salesman: Wait. What day is it?

Willie: It's Tuesday.

Salesman: It's Super Tuesday for our company, and I can offer you a Super Tuesday special price.

Willie: No, really. Thank you very much. Goodbye.

Salesman: Wait. Take a minute to reconsider. Didn't you say that you were wanting to find a good course? Well, here it is, and now it's 20 percent off if you order immediately.

Willie: Goodbye.

UNIT 9
Celebrating Success

Lesson 3, page 130

Narrator: In this interview Martha Bernard tries to focus on her skills, personal qualities that American employers want to see, and previous successes.

Ms. Koval: Hello, Ms. Bernard. My name is Helena Koval. Please . . . sit down.

Martha: Thank you, Ms. Koval. Here's my resume.

Ms. Koval: So, Ms. Bernard. What can you tell me about yourself? I see here that you've had no paid work experience as a cleaner.

Martha: Yes, that was my biggest concern when I decided to apply for this job. However, the responsibilities listed in your ad are exactly the same as ones I perform regularly in my home and also performed in a previous job when I worked as a home health aide.

Ms. Koval: Hmmm. I see. However, cleaning an office requires a lot more than vacuuming a small carpet. You might have some difficulties operating a heavy-duty commercial cleaner.

Martha: I know that there will be new things to learn on the job. But I'm a very fast learner. And I'm eager to develop new skills. As you can see from my resume, I have done volunteer jobs. I was required to learn new and unfamiliar skills.

Ms. Koval: Interesting. I must say that I am impressed by your resume, even though it is limited. I'm curious. Your volunteer experience was clerical and administrative. Why have you applied to work as a cleaner?

Martha: Your ad said that you would train me. And I like the flexible schedule, benefits, and opportunities for advancement.

Ms. Koval: Let me ask you some questions regarding your personal qualities. As you know from our ad, we want an honest worker. Can you tell me why that is important for someone who cleans offices and homes?

Martha: Well, when you clean somebody's office space, you may find personal belongings or important documents that should be left untouched. You may even find valuables that the employees have left around. I am completely trustworthy, and people and agencies have trusted me in the past. For example, I handled quite a lot of money as treasurer of my Parent's Association.

Ms. Koval: You've told me about your strengths. Now let's talk about your weaknesses.

Martha: People told me that as a volunteer I worked too hard. Sometimes that makes other workers look bad in front of their supervisors.

Ms. Koval: I know that problem from personal experience. OK . . . how would you handle a conflict with your colleagues at work?

Martha: I'd like to say that I'm quite competent at conflict resolution. I needed those skills in my position as Parent's Association treasurer. And, of course, being a parent has provided me with plenty of opportunities to practice conflict resolution. I believe that one way to stop a problem is to prevent it from starting. Being sensitive to my co-workers' needs, for example, may prevent unnecessary misunderstandings.

Ms. Koval: How do you react to criticism?

Martha: I try to learn from it. I believe that there is always something I can learn from both my superiors and my co-workers.

Ms. Koval: You've mentioned your child. Will your family responsibilities affect your work? We have a flexible schedule, but there are schedule demands, just like in any job.

Martha: I've planned my child care prior to this interview. I've also arranged for help in case of an emergency. Quite honestly, I don't expect to be absent from my job. You know, one feature of this job that appealed to me was the benefits it offers. I am sure that my family would do better if I had this job.

Ms. Koval: The fact that you have not worked with a supervisor worries me a little. I'm not sure how you would handle criticism and orders.

Martha: Of course, even as a volunteer, I had to follow orders. Even if I felt that things could be done differently, I respected the decisions of the organizers and worked cooperatively.

Ms. Koval: What do you see yourself doing five years from now?

Martha: I see myself working in a company like this, using my organizing skills as a supervisor of cleaners. I'd also like to learn sales skills. I'm good at that.

Ms. Koval: I can believe that. Frankly, I'm sold on your potential. You represent yourself very well. Of course, I need to check your references. What will they tell me about you?

Martha: That I'm a trustworthy person and a reliable one. Any job I start gets done.

Ms. Koval: Ms. Bernard, it was a pleasure interviewing you. I imagine that you'll hear from us within the next few days.

Martha: Thank you, Ms. Koval. I appreciate the time you've given me. I hope to hear from you soon. I know I'm a good worker, and I know that I can do good things at Elite.

Ms. Koval: Goodbye, Ms. Bernard.

Martha: Goodbye, Ms. Koval. Have a nice day now.

The US

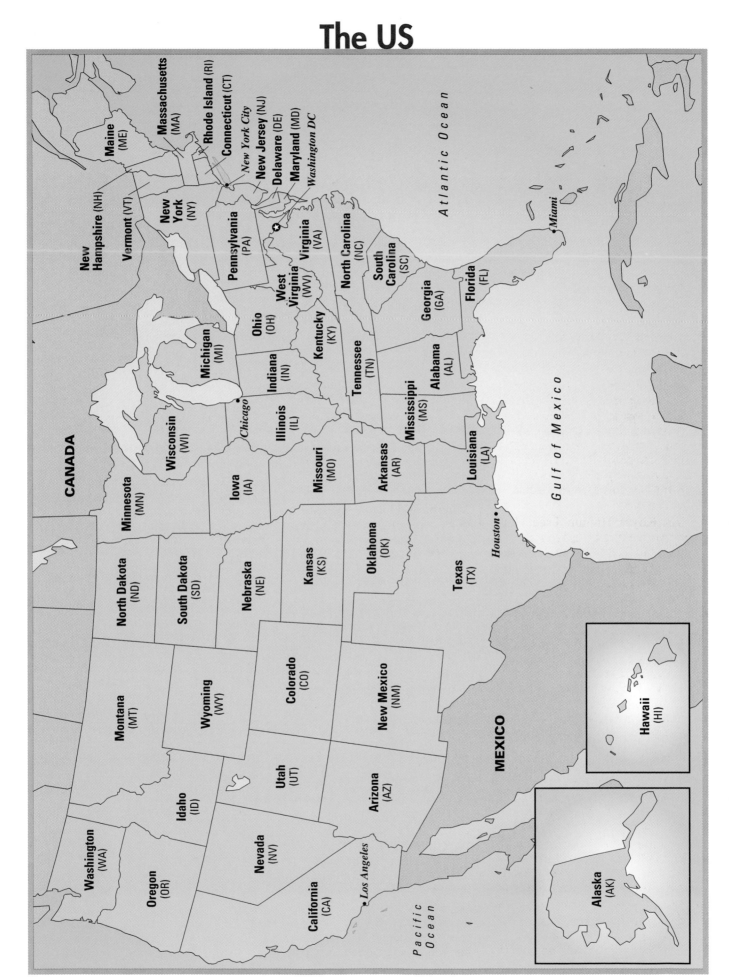

The World

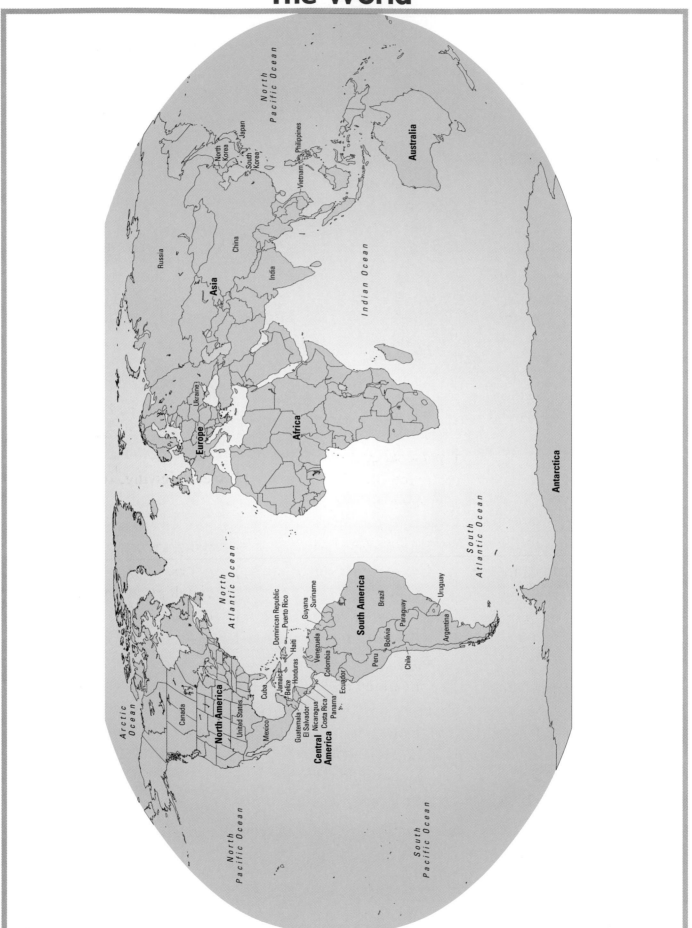

North Pacific Ocean

Russia

Asia

China

India

North Korea
South Korea
Japan

Vietnam
Philippines

Australia

Indian Ocean

Ukraine

Europe

Africa

Antarctica

Arctic Ocean

North Atlantic Ocean

South Atlantic Ocean

Canada

North America

United States

Mexico

Cuba

Jamaica
Belize
Honduras
Guatemala
El Salvador
Nicaragua
Costa Rica
Panama

Central America

Dominican Republic
Puerto Rico
Haiti

Guyana
Suriname
Venezuela
Colombia
Ecuador

South America

Brazil

Peru
Bolivia
Paraguay
Chile
Argentina
Uruguay

North Pacific Ocean

South Pacific Ocean

Topics

B

business customs in the US, 30

C

changing jobs in the US, 19

choices, making, 52–65

communication about difficult issues, 38–51

consumer issues, 66–79

contracts, written and verbal, in the US, 87

D

debating an issue, 56

democracy, participating in, 94–107

F

feelings, 24–37

G

getting professional help in the US, 47

goal-setting, 10–23

I

independence as a cultural value, 58

interviews, 24–37

J

job interviews, 122–135

L

learning at any age in the US, 114

learning styles, 119–120

learning, ways to learn, 108–121

legal terms, 80–93

listening scripts, 136–140

listening, active, 115

M

maps
  United States, 141
  world, 142

P

participating in a democracy, 94–107

personal qualities admired in the US, 128

problem-solving, 10–23

projects
  Create a Business, 65
  Create a Class Consumer Guide, 79
  Create a Personal Legal Glossary, 93
  Find Your Personal Learning Style, 121
  Make a Community Resource Guide, 107
  Make a Personal Achievement Record, 37
  Make a Resource Guide, 51
  Prepare a Resume, 135
  Write a Letter to Yourself from the Future, 23

R

researching
  organizations that offer help, 45, 48
  products, 73

resume, 122–135

S

safety, 52–65

self-reliance and involvement traditions in the US, 103

speech, giving, 108–121

T

talking about difficult issues, 38–51

technology and progress in the US, 75

V

voting procedures, 96–98

Grammar and Pronunciation

A

adjective clauses with *who,*
which, and *that,* 55
adverbs of time in past
perfect, 83
articles, 89

C

complex sentences, 61, 83
compound nouns,
pronunciation 72
compound sentences, 61
conditional contrary to fact,
27
connecting ideas with *so,*
because, and *although,* 61
could, should, and *would,*
pronunciation with *have,*
59

D

disappearing /h/, 103
disappearing sounds and
syllables, 117

E

embedded questions, 72

F

final consonants followed
by a vowel,
pronunciation, 44

G

gerunds, 89

I

indirect speech, 33
infinitives, 89
intonation
in statements, 19
with *yes/no* questions, 16

O

objects of prepositions, 41
of after a word ending in a
consonant, pronunciation,
41

P

passive voice in simple
present, 125
past continuous, 111
past participles, 69, 97
of irregular verbs, 100
past perfect, 16
compared with present
perfect, 16
adverbs of time in past
perfect, 83
past perfect continuous,
117
past tense, 13
compared with present
perfect, 13
prepositional phrases, 41,
44
prepositions of time *(on, in,*
at), 89
present and past participles
used as adjectives, 69, 97
present participles, 69, 97

present perfect, 13, 16
compared with simple
past, 13
compared with past
perfect, 16

R

reductions
could, should, and *would*
with *have,* 59
of after a word ending in
a consonant, 41

S

sounds
of *a* in *say, says, said,* 33
of consonant blends, 86
of diphthongs, 125
stress
in compound nouns, 72
in sentences, 30
of syllables affecting
word meaning, 128

T

-tion ending, pronunciation
58

V

verb tense review, 132

W

who, which, and *that* in
adjective clauses, 55